T0195820

MEDITATIONAL MOMENTS WITH GOD AND SERMONS FOR REFLECTION AND SPIRITUAL GROWTH

VOLUME II

Dr. Freddie A. Banks Jr.

authorHOUSE

AuthorHouse™
1663 Liberty Drive
Bloomington, IN 47403
www.authorhouse.com
Phone: 833-262-8899

Published by AuthorHouse 03/24/2021

ISBN: 978-1-6655-1998-4 (sc)
ISBN: 978-1-6655-1996-0 (hc)
ISBN: 978-1-6655-1997-7 (e)

Library of Congress Control Number: 2021905625

Print information available on the last page.

Scripture quotations marked RSV are taken from the Revised Standard Version of
the Bible, copyright © 1946, 1952, 1971 by the Division of Christian Education of
the National Council of the Churches of Christ in the USA. Used by permission.

Scripture quotations marked NIV are taken from the Holy Bible, New International
Version®. NIV®. Copyright © 1973, 1978, 1984 by International Bible
Society. Used by permission of Zondervan. All rights reserved. [Biblica]

Scripture quotations marked KJV are from the Holy Bible, King James Version
(Authorized Version). First published in 1611. Quoted from the KJV Classic
Reference Bible, Copyright © 1983 by The Zondervan Corporation.

This book is printed on acid-free paper.

Contents

Introduction ix

Acknowledgements xi

Dedication. xiii

Dedication

Jesus Is the Light of the World 1

When God Speaks – Listen 4

Money Worries Bring About Anxiety Versus Faith 9

From Misery to Praise Waiting on the Lord 12

Praying at Midnight 15

Exhortation to Obedience: Only God Can Save 18

Christ Condemns the Rebels for High Talk but Low Walk . . . 21

God's New Deal 24

Be a Living Sacrifice. 27

The Great Commission 30

How Can We Handle and Avoid Temptation? 33

Humbly Receive 36

Incomplete Obedience: Doing Almost All of God's Will.....39

The Consequences of Unbelief.........................41

Will You Be My Witness?.............................44

Your Struggle with Sin 46

Knowing Our Advent Themes 49

Thanksgiving Pardon Fellowship and Forgiveness 52

The Time is Now to Worship Him.....................55

Miraculous Escape 58

Ten Keys to God's Character 61

Obtaining the Peace of the Lord......................64

The Mercies of the Lord As We Have Hope In the Midst
of Suffering 67

God's Comfort for His People........................70

Knowing and Doing God's Will.......................72

Why Flee When You Can Trust?......................75

We Are Called to Be Different 78

Examine Yourselves.................................81

Stand Firm (Fast) in the Lord........................83

Facing Temptation: David's Fall......................86

Confession and Forgiveness 89

Is Faith Always Worthwhile?.........................92

If I'm Living Right, Then Why Do I Hurt So Much? 95

The Joy of Growing Up In Christ.....................98

Reflections

God's Way or No Way.............................101

The Institution of Marriage God's Plan for Marriage
When One Plus One Equals One 107
Total Trust. 114
Is God Really in Your Life First?. 117

Sermons

Dr. Gloria Bledsoe Cox, Biography. 121
The Fixer. 123
You Go-and Wake the Town and Tell the People. 130
God Chooses Just Plain Ordinary People to Serve Him. 137
Ordinary People 147
Understanding the Provisions of God. 149
The Lord Gives and The Lord Takes Away 158
Do You have a Passion for His Presence? 171

About the Book. 185
About the Author. 187

Introduction

When we are faced with the challenges of everyday, we as believers may sometimes feel that God is far away from us. We at times feel that our flourishing faith life is withering away when the problems and difficulties of life beset us. However, we can be reassured that God, through his word, is present with us, in all aspects of our lives, even in the most unexpected difficult circumstances and situations.

Why yet another book on Meditational Moments with God and Sermons with God? The reason is because that is the nature of scripture which is always given into interpretation. We must remember that the task of the Minister, is to bring new, fresh, insights to the old story. My purpose in writing this book was to evirate the reader in serious thought and meditation regarding various scriptures and meditations and to prompt the questions, what do these words mean? More importantly, what do they mean to me? In addition to this, a series of meditations are presented that are designed to help the reader learn to think theologically about life issues; and to help the reader strengthen their faith in God who does all things well and most importantly to enable them to grow in their relationships with God.

The study of these meditations and sermons is intentionally and invitational. As you read and study these materials, you are asked to give prayerfully consideration to your own relationship to Jesus Christ and make or renew your commitment, to offer your spoken prayers, and to pray with and for others. If you do this you will grow more confident with prayer and with your covenant relationship with the Lord Jesus Christ.

This book contains a collection of meditations and sermons which are designed to inspire, comfort, console, and help the reader enhance his or her walk with the Lord Jesus Christ as they face the day to day challenges of life. We pray that you will find a blessing in them.

Acknowledgements

I want to first acknowledge with thanks and appreciation the students at Eastern Illinois University and the members of Samuel Brown Temple A.M.E Zion Church, St. Louis Missouri, who first heard my sermons and meditations. It was my desire as a minister of the gospel to have a listening congregation, those who listened with their mind, heart, and soul. For 22 years, I was blessed with such a congregation.

Then to Denean Vaughn, who has prepared my books, including this one for publication. She and her skills, subtle, pertinent and persistent were as essential to this process as food is to the body. For these and all her many kindnesses, I am sincerely grateful.

Then to Tukesha Harris, a special thanks who painstakingly helped prepare this manuscript for publication. She has undertaken the proofreading and the editing work with a rare dedication and competence that is difficult to find. I know she did it with a tremendous amount of love. Thanks so very much for your labor of love.

Then to my friends and members of my extended family who have received my works with such patience and encouragements were participants in this venture. I thank my God upon every remembrance of you.

Dedication

This book is dedicated in loving memory of my parents, John Ella Parm-Banks and Freddie Augustus Banks, Sr. who removed the stumbling blocks and taught me how to be strong and survival. May their spirits continue to grow in me.

To my wife, Roselena (Rosebud), how can I say thanks to you for the things you have done for me during the writing of this book? You have provided nurturing for our children, grandchildren, and even our great-grandchildren; and yet you continue to be a partner in ministry these 27 years. On this journey, a journey that only a few have found, I want you to know that because of your passion, you have made this journey sweeter and your tenderness is like a rainbow in the sky after a storm. So, when I think about the journey and when I look at you, I know heaven is missing an angel, because I have one walking with me. Thank you for being my partner and my supporter- my precious jewel.

To my children, Curtis, Maurice, TyTanisha, Yashika, and Booker. May this book be a source of inspiration to you throughout your lives.

To my grandchildren, Celeste, Emani, Tajai, Channing, Mashayla, Abril, Havyn and Brooke. May the contents of this book be an inspiration to you.

To my great-grandchildren, Aniyah Jasmine, and Mackenzie. May the content of this book be an inspiration to you.

Jesus Is the Light of the World

John 8: 12-20

Jesus never spoke in public without creating some controversy. In fact, he was constantly in trouble. But rather than retreating behind the safety of a pulpit, Jesus spoke in settings where people were bold enough to talk back. In this portion of John's story, Jesus makes a series of claims about himself. Each claim is met by a challenge from his enemies. Each challenge is then answered, and the answer leads to the next claim. Throughout this exchange, Jesus shows us how to speak the truth in the face of hostility, as he reveals some amazing things about himself.

Then spake Jesus again unto them saying, "I am the light of the world: he that followeth me shall not walk in darkness, but shall have the light of life." In this scripture, the scene shifts to the treasury of the temple. A multitude was still following Jesus. He turned to them and made one of the many grand statements as to his Messiahship. He said, "I am the light of the world." Naturally speaking the world is in the darkness of sin, ignorance, and aimlessness. The light of the world is Jesus. Apart from him, there is no deliverance from the blackness of sin. Apart from him there is no guidance and direction along the way of life, apart from him there is no life, for he is the way, the truth and the life and the issue of eternity. Jesus has promised that anyone following him would not walk in darkness, but have the light. For apart from him we have no knowledge as to the real meaning of life and the issue of eternity. We must realize that to follow Jesus means to believe in him. Many people have the mistaken idea that they can live as Jesus lived without ever being born again. To follow Jesus means to come to him in repentance, to trust him as Lord and Savior and then to commit your whole life to him. Those who do this will have guidance in life and bright hope beyond the grave. Throughout this interchange Jesus shows us how to speak the truth in the face of hostility. We as ambassador of God should always speak the truth whenever the opportunity comes, for Jesus is the light of the world.

Focus Scripture: John 8:12-14

"Then spake Jesus again unto them, saying, I am the light of the world: he that followeth me shall not walk in darkness, but shall have the light of life. The Pharisees therefore said unto him, Thou bearest record of thyself; thy record is not true. Jesus answered and said unto them, Though I bear record of myself, yet my record is true: for I know whence I came, and whither I go; but ye cannot tell whence I come, and whither I go."

Focus Questions:

The Pharisees challenge the validity of Jesus claim, how then does Jesus answer their challenge? Jesus then references to his father leads to a second claim, which was that he came from God. Briefly explain how this claim heightens the tension between Jesus and the Jews?

Meditations Points to Ponder:

Briefly explain why the conduct that we exhibit daily is the truest test of our belief? Then think about how does your lifestyle validate or invalidate your claim to being a follower of Christ? Have you ever tried to talk about Christ with a family member or coworker who was hostile to your message? How did you feel at the time?

When God Speaks – Listen

Genesis 3:7-19

Through the ages, God has talked with authority because he is the great creator of the vast universe and everything therein. When he speaks, mankind should listen. The voice of God was heard first by progenitors of the human race in the garden of Eden who heard the voice of the Lord God in the cool of the day. The Lord called unto Adam and said unto him, "Where art thou?"

Adam and Eve, although created innocent and holy, were placed in the perfect environment but not placed beyond the possibility of sin. However, it was the desire of the Lord that this pair should remain in the state of blissful obedience.

Their standing in the midst of a luxuriant garden was the tree of knowledge of good and evil. It was to be a test of obedience, love and faith to our first parents. They were forbidden to taste the fruit of this tree. Of course, God could have made man without the power to disobey His divine law. He could have made it impossible for Adam and Eve to touch the forbidden fruit, but man was not to be a mere puppet without the freedom of choice. No – to the contrary. I believe God wanted man to be a free moral agent with the power of choice. There was no other way to develop character in human intelligence except to grant to the first man and woman the power to choose, obey and disobey. They could obey and live or disobey and die.

As the story unfolds, Eve was deceived by Satan and she partook of the forbidden fruit. She then offered it to Adam who ate too. The garment of innocence left them, and they were naked about this time, God called them. Because of sin, they were horrified and darted behind the foliage to hide themselves in the presence of God. In the ensuing dialogue which follows, Adam, whose love for his companion had outweighed his love and loyalty to God, now blamed her for the predicament, stating coldly, "This woman whom Thou gavest to be with me, she gave me of the tree, and I did eat." (Genesis 3:12) In a prompt rebuttal, Eve blamed the serpent who had deceived her. Adam, on the other hand, admitted that this disobedience had been deliberate and willful. God spoke to the serpent and declared, "Because thou has done this, thou art cursed above all cattle and above all beasts of the field. Upon thy belly thy shall go and you, shall eat dust all the days of thy life." (Genesis 3:14)

God's voice continued and unto the woman he said, "I will greatly multiply thy sorrow and by conception and sorrow, thou shalt bring for the children and thou desire shall be to thy husband and he shall rule over thee." (Genesis 3:16) Turning to the first man, the Lord said, "Cursed is the ground for thy sake and then sorrow shall thou eat all the days of thy life in the sweat of thou face, shall thou eat bread until thou return to the ground. For out of it, thou was taken and dust though art and unto dust thou shall be returned." The Lord was showing to Adam and Eve the sacredness of his love and wanted them, by their own experience, to see the danger of setting aside even in the slightest degree. In this generation, god is speaking again. I believe He is asking all of us in all of our churches, all of us who are Christian – "Where art thou?" Would we have to hide ourselves like Adam and Eve, from His presence? If not, would he find us working in the church and the community for the up building of His kingdom here on earth? Are we keeping his commandments or are we demonstrating a Christ-like spirit of forgiveness in dealing with our fellow man? Do we really love our neighbors? Are we optimistic about life? Indeed, God is talking today through His word. He is calling all of us from sin to righteousness and from death to life through faith in His son, Jesus Christ. (Isaiah 55:1, John 3:16) He is proclaiming a message of hope to a hopeless world and when he speaks, we are to listen. We are to put aside sometimes that small talk of the little small member. For you know, there is such a small member in our bodies, a muscle called the tongue. But what a magnitude of good can be wrought by it likewise, what a great deal of evil can be proclaimed by it. The tongue was formed by an all knowing and loving God for many purposes. Though small, it was to be of great importance. Even so, the tongue can cause another person to withdraw or become hurt when it lashes out in a scolding manner. Many of us use our tongues for fault finding, relating other's shortcomings and failures. Passing on a juicy bit of gossip and even telling a true event in sordid details just to leave others feeling gloomy and worthless. If you think about it, the wrong use of our tongue can inject a great deal of poison into another. It can even be destructive if we allow it. On the other hand, speaking words of encouragement, talking about the good in others, relating happy experiences and telling an unsaved person about the savior are all a means of increasing and uplifting a person. A little tongue this day can start someone on the downward journey of death or that same tongue can encourage one to prepare for eternal life. Let us heed today to the use we make of that small member of ours for it will bear fruit and they that use it as well as they that did hear it, shall eat of the fruit. His word is calling us to use every member and use it wisely.

Focus Scripture: Genesis 3

"Now the serpent was more crafty than any of the wild animals the Lord God had made. He said to the woman, "Did God really say, 'You must not eat from any tree in the garden?" The woman said to the serpent, "We may eat fruit from the trees in the garden, but God did say, "You must not eat fruit from the tree that is in the middle of the garden, and you must not touch it, or you will die." "You will not certainly die," the serpent said to the woman. "For God knows that when you eat from it your eyes will be opened, and you will be like God, knowing good and evil." When the woman saw that the fruit of the tree was good for food and pleasing to the eye, and also desirable for gaining wisdom, she took some and ate it. She also gave some to her husband, who was with her, and he ate it. Then the eyes of both of them were opened, and they realized they were naked; so they sewed fig leaves together and made coverings for themselves."

Focus Questions:

How does Eve misrepresent God's command? How have the serpent's words distorted Eve's thinking?

Meditation Points to Ponder:

Adam and Eve made several mistakes; they listened to a creature instead of God, followed their own impressions against Gods instructions, doubted God's concern for their best interests and made self-fulfillment of their goal. In what situation have any of these led you to disobey a command of God? What lesson have you learned from this study that can help you recognize and resist temptations you are facing?

Money Worries Bring About Anxiety Versus Faith

Luke 12:22-31

One of the great dangers in the Christian Life is that the acquisition of food and clothing become the first and foremost aim of our existence. We become so occupied with earning money for these things that the work of the Lord is relegated to a secondary place. The emphasis of the New Testament is that the cause of Christ should have first place in our lives. Food and clothing should be subordinate. We should work hard for the supply of our current necessities, then trust God for the future as we plunge ourselves into God's service for this is the life of faith. Of his words recorded in the Bible, Jesus has more to say on money than any other topic. Luke 12 offers a good summary of his attitude. He (God) does not condemn possessions, but he warns against putting faith in money to secure the future. Money fails to solve life's big problems.

Although Jesus speaks to many aspects on the question of money, he seems to concentrate on the question: What is money doing to you? Money can dominate a person's life, diverting attention away from God. Jesus challenges us to break free of money's power even if it means giving it all away. Jesus urges his listeners to seek treasures in the kingdom of God, for such treasure can benefit them in this life and the next one too. Don't worry, he says in verse 22 for God is the one who provides for our needs. Then to emphasize his point, he brings up King Solomon, the richest man in the Old Testament. Jesus said that a common wildflower is clothed more gloriously by god than a royal king. So do not have an anxious mind, "but seek the kingdom of God and all things will be added to you." It is better to trust God who lavishes care on the whole earth than to spend our lives worrying about money and possessions. For if we seek the kingdom, he will never let us starve or be naked, for God never intended his people should spend their time in the mad rush for creatures' comforts.

Focus Scripture: Luke 12:22-23

"And he said unto his disciples, Therefore I say unto you, take no thought for your life, what ye shall eat; neither for the body, what ye shall put on. The life is more than meat, and the body is more than raiment."

Focus Questions:

Nowhere does Jesus condemn processions, but he has a lot to say about how to use them. How could you as one of his servants summarize Jesus' teaching about life and material goods (money)? What view of God does worrying Christians have?

Meditations Points to Ponder:

The obviously rich are not the only ones in danger of being fools. How do poor and middle-class people also face dangers? Recall again in your mind your past week's activities and personal concerns. To what extent do they reflect the priorities and values of God's kingdom?

From Misery to Praise
Waiting on the Lord

1 Samuel 1: 9-20

And she was in bitterness of soul, and prayed unto the Lord, and wept. Hannah vowed that if God would give her a male child, she would give him back to the Lord. He would be a Nazarite from birth. Someone said the way to obtain any benefit is to dedicate it in our hearts to the glory of that God of whom we ask it. By this means shall God both please his servant and honor himself. Waiting is one of the hardest things we do. So much of our life involves waiting and in an age of instant products, waiting irritates us. But waiting is hardest when we see the clock running on, the years going by and still our hopes and dreams are about waiting. In our text, Hannah knew about waiting. Living in a society that measured a woman's worth by her children, Hannah was barren. Year after year she waited in misery for the answer to her prayer. She had two choices to be bitter or to continue seeking God's help.

This quiet time Bible looks at Hannah's journey from misery to praise. What Hannah did was to continue to pray to the Lord. The old priest, Eli, saw Hannah's lips moving and supposed her to be drunk. But as she explained her actions, he perceived her seriousness; he blessed her, and sent her on her way in peace. Hannah was concerned about her physical barrenness. We shall mourn our spiritual barrenness. When Hannah's prayer was answered, she named her baby Samuel (heard of God) because he was asked from the Lord. When Samuel was weaned, she took him to the house of the Lord and sent him to the house in a once for all act of dedication. What cherished hope or dream do you increasingly fear may never be realized in your life? Whatever it is you must pray to God openly about it, expect it to happen and promise God something for answered prayer.

Focus Scripture: 1 Samuel 1:10-11, 19

"And she was in bitterness of soul, and prayed unto the LORD, and wept sore. And she vowed a vow, and said, O LORD of hosts, if thou wilt indeed look on the affliction of thine handmaid, and remember me, and not forget thine handmaid, but wilt give unto thine handmaid a man child, then I will give him unto the LORD all the days of his life, and there shall no razor come upon his head. Wherefore it came to pass, when the time was come about after Hannah had conceived, that she bare a son, and called his name Samuel, saying, because I have asked him of the LORD."

Focus Question:

Hannah turns to God in desperation, what does her prayer reveal about her life to you? Find several strong beliefs that Hannah believes about God. If you were describing Hannah to a loved one or friend, what would you say about her, her gifts and her spiritual life?

Meditation Points to Ponder:

Have you ever been bitter about your disappointments, what did you do and to whom did you turn to? What specific things can you learn from Hannah about the solutions to the pain of unfilled hopes, dreams, or desires?

Praying at Midnight

Acts 16:25

And at midnight Paul and Silas prayed and sang praise unto god: and the prisoners heard them. (Acts 16:25)

It appears that trouble will intensify or eliminate your prayer life. By that I mean, that difficulties have a way of proving to us how much we truly trust God we solicit in prayer. The indisputable truth is important because midnight is in all of our lives. Each of us will be required to experience the midnight of failing health, the midnight of family bereavement, the midnight of economic distress and the midnight of misunderstanding, but the passage reminds us that the God who answers in the morning, at midday, is also the God who answers at midnight. Let me set the stage for you.

Paul and Silas are in a prison because they cast a spirit out of fortune telling of a native girl there in Philippi. Now, one would expect Paul and Silas to be bitter because of the experience, but they found joy in the suffering for the cause of Christ. They found so much joy that they conducted a prison devotional service.

The text does not indicate that they began singing at midnight, but that at midnight they continued the devotion that had been done earlier. They filled the prison with hymns and prayers providing a spiritual unction to the usual business of prison. The prayer meeting was so powerful that God was moved to shake the prison with an earthquake. When the jailer saw the prison had been shaken open by the powerful earthquake, he intended to kill himself. But Paul called out to the jailer to not harm himself because no prisoner had left. I find it interesting that out of all the people justly incarcerated for crimes against the Roman code of conduct, none of them sought to leave. The spiritual freedom that was present as a result of Paul and Silas' prayer meeting meant more to them than the natural freedom they would have ascertained if they had fled the prison.

Perhaps, they sang "What A Friend We Have In Jesus" or "Father, I Stretch My Hands To Thee, No Other Help I Know" or "His Eye Is On The Sparrow" or "Precious Lord Take My Hand." But the songs of faith shook the prison walls.

When we faithfully pray during the midnights of our lives, we offer an opportunity for others to be blessed by the ministry that we display. It is through the troubling moments of our lives that God is glorified. For the testing of our faith not only allows us to develop patience, but it also gives us an opportunity and a testimony. God is best glorified not in the tranquil moments of our lives, but rather in the tempestuous moments of our existence. Regardless of what life hands you, take each midnight as an opportunity to prayerfully glorify God that humanity may seek to develop a stronger relationship with the God that you love. For we live in a world that is filled with pain and problems. We exist in a reality that seeks to drive Christ from within us. Glorifying God is not optional for the sincere Christian; it is a must. We have been saved to save others; your midnight revival is essential to their salvation.

Our prayer should be, dear God we thank thee for the midnight moments in our lives. We are grateful that you trust us with difficult situations. May we glorify you while in the midst of the crucible of conflict in such a way that all humanity will come to know you as Savior and Lord in the name of Jesus we pray. For the word of God, for the people of God, thanks be to God.

Focus Scripture: Acts 16:25

"And at midnight Paul and Silas prayed and sang praise unto God: and the prisoners heard them. Suddenly there was such a violent earthquake that the foundations of the prison were shaken. At once all the prison doors flew open, and everyone's chains came loose."

Focus Question:

How does your response to opposition and to suffering for the gospel compare to or contrast with that of Paul and Silas?

Meditation Points to Ponder:

Paul and Silas speak the truth of the gospel as well as living it out. How do you give both a verbal and a living witness to Jesus? Is there a person or task to which God is calling you? What steps do you need to take for immediate and unreserved obedience?

Exhortation to Obedience: Only God Can Save

Deuteronomy 4:15-30

Sometimes I think we forget what Christianity is all about. In the midst of Bible studies, worship service, church, board meetings, committee duties, and service projects, we end up just going through the motions. I believe that somehow the Christian faith collapses into a set of obligations that we are required to fulfill and a set of activities that we are supposed to be doing. Then as the sunlight coming through the clouds, the central truth breaks through. We are reminded that God is a saving God, he is a liberating God, and he is a God who wants freedom for his people. In this scripture Moses rehearsal of the law, as he dealt particularly with the worship of one true God and with the penalties that would follow any turning to idolatry. The passage that you are about to read is one you need to fix in your mind and read it from time to time. For it summarizes the central message of the Bible. God took his people from slavery in Egypt to freedom. There is no one like him. When that shift takes place in my mind, the pressures of obligation changes to gratitude and heartfelt service. What we need to do is to take our obligations regarding church, work, family, and commit them to the Lord's keeping and then sit in quiet for a few moments and practice gratitude for the freedom that he (God) brings. Practice being obedient children in your service and love for God. Then see God grow in your life.

Focus Scripture: Deuteronomy 4:23-24

"Take heed unto yourselves, lest ye forget the covenant of the LORD your God, which he made with you, and make you a graven image, or the likeness of anything, which the LORD thy God hath forbidden thee. For the LORD thy God is a consuming fire, even a jealous God."

Focus Questions:

What are the different types of idolatry that the people are warned against and what are the results of idolatry? What had God done to achieve Israel's salvation, what should be Israel's response to God's saving works?

Meditation Points to Ponder:

Think about it, for Israel, one of the gifts coming with their salvation was the Promised Land, but what are some of the benefits that come to Christians through Christ's achievement of salvation on the cross? Now what can you do to keep from taking your salvation for granted as Israel was in danger of doing?

Christ Condemns the Rebels for High Talk but Low Walk

Matthew 23:1-26

Influence is a powerful force in our lives. Those who influence others are able to change minds and to direct action. In today's lesson the religious leaders in Israel possessed the power to influence, especially on the new young converts. After they decided to oppose Jesus, they tried to lead others to do the same. In Matthew 23, Jesus condemns them point-blank, the Savior warns the crowds and his disciples against the scribes and the Pharisees. These leaders sat in Moses seat, or taught the Law of Moses. Generally, their teachings were dependable, but their practice was not. Their creed was better than their conduct. It was a case of high talk and low walk. So, Jesus said, "Whatever they tell you to observe, that observe and do, but do not do according to their works, for they say, and do not do."

They should have been the first to enter the kingdom because of their knowledge of scripture and their standing in the Jewish community. Because they refused. Jesus calls them to judgment. This passage exposes the guilt of those who do not practice what they preach. So if you have been hurt by inconsistency in the life or teaching of an influential person you respected, talk to God about your feelings of hurt and ask God to make your Christian life consistent with your beliefs and they will walk the talk you believe. For it is a declaration of the essential relations of man to God. There are three things which constitute a Christian, what he is, what he believes, and what he does; doctrine, experience, and practice. Man needs for his spiritual being three things, life, instruction, guidance; just what our Lord declares in the ten words of the gospel, "I am the way, and the truth, and the life." "Acknowledge no man as father, for no man can impact or sustain spiritual life; install no man as an infallible teacher; allow no one to assume the office of spiritual director; your relation to God and to Christ as close as that of any person." Live what you talk about, not by words but of your life. Christ condemns the rebels for high talk but low walk; good doctrine, but evil examples of life. "You are to be ye doers of the word not hearers only." Practice what you preach.

Focus Scripture: Matthew 23:1-3

"Then Jesus spake to the multitude, and disciples, saying the scribes and the Pharisees sit in Moses seat: All therefore whatsoever they bid you observe, that observe and do; but do not ye after their works: for they say, and do not."

Focus Question:

What attitude does Jesus teach the people to have toward the religious leaders and why? Compare the motives of the religious leaders with the motives and attitudes Jesus requires of his followers.

Meditation Points to Ponder:

Our Lord and Savior Jesus Christ condemns the religious leaders for confusing inward and outward righteousness. In what ways are we inclined to do that today? Where does this point out a place that needs to change in your life. How can you make your Christian life more consistent with your beliefs?

God's New Deal

Hebrews 8:1-13

Back in 1932, President Roosevelt sought to rescue the country from the Pitt of the Great Depression by launching the New Deal. The concept caught the imagination of the American people. The time was ripe for a radically new economic social program. Well in this chapter, the writer of Hebrews announces God's "New Deal", a new covenant, or agreement, between God and humanity. First there is a comparison of Christ ministry to the old one.

The second covenant is better because it is enacted on better promises. Christ's ministry is infinitely better. He offered himself, not an animal. He presented the value of his own blood, not the blood of bulls and goats. He put away sins, not merely covered them. He gave believers a perfect conscience, not an annual reminder of sins. He opened the way for us to enter into the presence of God, not to stand outside at a distance. He is also mediator of a better covenant. He stands between God and man to bridge the gap of estrangement. The covenant is better because it is absolute and not conditional, spiritual not carnal, universal, not local, eternal not temporal, individual not national and internal not external.

It is better because it is founded on better promises. The covenant of law promised blessings for obedience and threatened death for disobedience. It required righteousness but did not give the ability to produce it. The New Deal covenant is an unconditional covenant of grace. It imputes righteousness where there is none. It teaches men to live righteously, empowers them to do so, and rewards them when they do. Listen to the word as it distinguishes between the old (Deal) covenant and the new (Deal) government. And be thankful for the new covenant which is recited from beginning to end of what God agrees to do, this is its strength.

Focus Scripture: Hebrews 8:1-13

"For this is the covenant that I will make with the house of Israel after those days, saith the Lord; I will put my laws into their minds, and write them in their hearts; and I will be to them a God, and they shall be to me a people."

Focus Questions:

What was the problem with the first covenant? (v.7-12) What guarantees God's New Deal? What happens to you the Christian when you say to God, thank you Lord for forgiving and forgetting my sin?"

Meditation Points to Ponder:

Do you the believer function better under external restraints, the law or inner constraints, God's spirit and why? What does knowing that you are God's child mean to you?

Be a Living Sacrifice

Romans 12:1-10

The thing we need to know is that sacrifice is still a part of the Christian's life. To get something we are still going to have to make some sacrifices. Then what is sacrifice? It is something that cost us something. It is something we give up, even though it means something to us.

It is something we cannot part with easily or lightly. It is something we think twice about before we give it up. It entails denying ourselves of something because of our love and desire for something else. Therefore, we love God more than anything or anybody, he comes first. If we can easily give up something without much thought, then it is not a true sacrifice.

If we can give it up and walk away from it without a second thought, it is not a sacrifice. If it is something we do not have to struggle with, prayer and agonize over it before we part with it, it is not a sacrifice. It if is something that we won't miss, or if after giving it up we don't feel it in our heads, hearts, or our pocketbooks, it is not a sacrifice.

We must sacrifice the understanding and support of close friends, family, and supporters in order to achieve your goal. You must sacrifice short-term comfort for long-term gains. For the ideas of sacrifice is not popular. In a world of instant this and instant that, in a world of mass marketing fame and glory, in a world of charge it now and pay later, in a world of casual sex and broken vows, or in a world where the right contacts are considered to be more important than the right education or the right morals, or the right works; sacrifice is not popular.

But the last time I read the Bible the word "sacrifice" like the word "discipline" like the word "truth," like the word "honest," like the word "obedience," like the word "tithe," like the word "give," was still there, that tells me that sacrifice is till part of the Christian life. So, to get something in life we are still going to have to make some sacrifices.

In essence, Jesus had to make a sacrifice, he looked beyond temptations and the comfort and support that were in front of him and chose the cross. To the distress of the devil, to the dismay of the crowds, to the disappointment of friends and family, he chose death on the cross. He sacrificed present friends and family for a future promise. He sacrificed short term rewards for long-term righteousness and gain. Know this, it may not be popular to say, but the truth is you don't get much of anywhere in life, and even if you get there, you don't stay very long or enjoy it very much, without some sacrifice.

Lastly, know this when you are out there seemly by yourself, when nobody seems to understand, and those who do understand are not able to help you, you know beyond the shadow of a doubt that God is with you and God will see you through. Just remain faithful unto God and he will be faithful to you and God rewards those who makes sacrifices to pursue God's vision and will for their lives.

"Therefore, present your body a living sacrifice holy and acceptable unto God, which is your reasonable service. Then take up the cross, deny yourself and follow him and find life even as you walk alone."

Focus Scripture: Romans 12:1

"I beseech you therefore brethren by the mercies of God, that you present your bodies a living sacrifice, holy, acceptable unto God, which is your reasonable service."

Focus Questions:

How does the imagery of living sacrifices describe our proper response to God's mercy, his grace and love toward us?

Meditation Points to Ponder:

List and explain some ways that we can renew our minds and be transformed. Then take a moment and think with sober judgment about yourself. What gifts do you think God has given you to use for Christ then ask God to use you in serving the body of Christ with your gifts?

The Great Commission

Matthews 28:16-20

In Galilee, the risen Lord Jesus appeared to his disciples at an unnamed mountain. His sufferings were passed forever. Because he lived, they too would live. He had completed the work of redemption. As head of the new creation, he then issued the Great Commission, containing "Stand Orders" for all believers. The Great Commission contains three commands, not suggestions:

1. "Go therefore and make disciples of all nations. This does not presuppose word conversion. By preaching the gospel, the disciples were to see others become learners of followers of the Savior from every nation, people, and tongue.
2. "Baptize "them in the name of the Father and of the Son and of the Holy Spirit." The responsibility rests on Christ's messengers to teach baptism, and to press it as a command to be obeyed. In believer's baptism, Christians publicly identify themselves with the triune Godhead. They

acknowledge that God is their Father, that Jesus Christ is their Lord and Savior and that the Holy Spirit is the one who indwells, empowers and teaches them.

3. Teach "them to observe all things that I have commanded you." The commission goes beyond evangelism, it is not enough to simply make converts and let them fend for themselves. They must be taught to obey the commandments of Christ as found in the New Testament the essence of discipleship is becoming like the master and this is brought about by systematic teaching and submission to the word then the Savior added a promise of his presence with his disciples until the emanation of the age. They would not go forth alone or unaided. In all their service and travel they would know the companionship of the son of God. The task is still uncompleted. What are you doing to carry out his command?

Focus Scripture: Matthew 28:16-20

"Go ye therefore, and teach all nations, baptizing them in the name of the Father, and of the Son, and of the Holy Ghost: Teaching them to observe all things whatsoever I have commanded you: and, lo, I am with you always, even unto the end of the world."

Focus Questions:

As you recall the joy of Easter celebration that you have experienced, what elements made that joy for you? The disciples go to Galilee where they meet with Jesus. Describe the commission he gave to them and to us? How does Jesus equip them and future disciples to carry out his commission?

Meditation Points to Ponder:

From you point of view what keeps people today from believing that Jesus is the resurrected Lord? As you end you study of Matthew, how can you become more involved in making disciples and fulfilling the great commission?

How Can We Handle and Avoid Temptation?

Genesis 3:1-19

Why did God make man so that he could sin or if God is good and powerful, why does he allow so much evil and pain. Well is there any other way he could have made us? Could there be a moral creature without the power to choose? Freedom is God's gift to man: Freedom to think, freedom of conscience, even though man uses his freedom to face temptation and to obey or disobey God is his choice. Although the Bible doesn't answer this question directly, it shows how sin and its consequences entered the world. In the last chapter we left Adam and Eve in Eden at peace with God, themselves and the natural world over which they had been given stewardship. They had freedom to fulfill this responsibility and eat any fruit in the garden, with one exception. The tree of knowledge of good and evil would be the test of their obedience to God it was their choice. In this study we see how they faced sin and temptation, how they met this test and what lessons we could learn from their experience. A story is told about a certain train wreck, the engineer, who could have saved his life by jumping, stuck to his post, and save the passengers, but lost his own life. They erected a monument, not to the train, for it did only what its machinery forced it to do, but to the engineer, who of his own volition, chose to give his life to save passengers. What virtue is there in obeying God if in our nature there is no inclination to do otherwise? But if our own choice, and against the steady urge of our nature, we obey God, there is character in that. Remember that no temptation or sin is any different or worse than the first sin in the Garden of Eden and only he can forgive and save. Let us always remember that we can avoid temptation by being obedient to the word of God by following the Holy Spirit as it speaks to us and you need to know that no sin is any different or worse than the sin of Adam and Even in the Garden of Eden. However, there is hope simply by telling it to Jesus and then allow him to forgive you.

Focus Scripture: Genesis 3:3

"But of the fruit of the tree which is in the midst of the garden, God hath said, ye shall not eat of it neither shall ye touch it, least ye die."

Focus Question:

Briefly explain how answering to Satan misrepresented God's command. What statements does Satan make about the purpose and results of the command given to Eve by God? In verses 4-5, explain. There is always a consequence for our sinful behavior, what judgments did the Lord pronounce upon Adam, Eve, and the serpent?

Meditation Points to Ponder:

Adam and Eve made several mistakes. They listened to Satan instead of the God who created them, they then followed their own perceptions and impressions against God's instruction; and they doubted God's concern for their own best interests and made self-fulfillment their goal. What lessons have you received from this study that will enable you to recognize and resist temptations that you face daily?

Humbly Receive

James 1: 13-22

While reading the first chapter of James, I was struck by the phrase, "Humbly accept the word planted in you, which can save you (21)." A decision with which I had been struggling with came to my mind, and I thought I don't need to read another book, attend another seminar, or ask another friend about this. I just need to obey what the Bible tells me to do. My efforts to be better informed had become a means of resisting God's destruction rather than receiving it. James was writing to followers of Christ when he said, "Lay aside all filthiness and overflow of wickedness and receive with meekness the implanted word which is able to save your souls. But be ye doers of the word, and not hearers only, deceiving yourself." (James 1:21-22). Bible scholar, W.E. Vine said that the Greek word used here for received means "deliberate and ready reception of what is offered." Meekness is an attitude toward God in which we accept his dealings with us as good, and therefore without disputing or resisting a humble heart doesn't fight against

God or contend with him. God's powerful word implanted in our hearts is a trustworthy source of spiritual wisdom and strength. It is available to all who will humbly receive it. God, who formed worlds by the power of his word, speaks through the scriptures so his truth will be heard. If we read it, with the will to obey, he by his spirit will show us the way. So, we must open our bibles prayerfully, read it carefully, and obey it joyfully.

We must remember that it is all too possible to read the Bible without letting it speak to us. We can study it in an academic way without being affected by it. Sometimes our pride, hardiness and sin make us unreceptive and unresponsive to the word. However, only those with submissive, humble spirits can expect to derive the maximum benefits from the scriptures. For it is the humble that he guides in justice, and the humble he teaches his way. "But on this one I will look: on him who is poor and of a contrite spirit, and who trembles at my word." (Isaiah 66:2) So, James speaks of the scripture as the implanted word, which is able to save your souls. The thought is that the word becomes a sacred deposit in the Christians' life when he/she is born again. Then the word is able to save your soul. Notice that the bible is the instrument God uses in the New Birth. He uses it in saving the soul not only from the penalty of sin, but also from sins power as well. He uses it in saving us not only from damnation in eternity, but also from damage in this life for it is doubtless this present, continuing aspect of salvation James is speaking of in verse 21. Therefore, it is not enough to receive the implanted word, we must obey it. The ideal combination is to read the word and obey it implicitly.

Focus Scripture: James 1:13-22

"Wherefore, put away all filthiness and overflowing of wickedness, and receive with meekness the engrafted word which is able to save your soul."

Focus Question:

James words tell us that God's words were planted in us. Briefly explain that we can choke that word and keep it from growing and humbly accepting the word planted in you, which can save you? Based on what you have read in this chapter, do you believe James would be satisfied with good works apart from our listening to and receiving God's word?

Meditation Points to Ponder:

When is it difficult for you to listen to God? However, sometimes we do listen to God's word, but we still don't follow it. Is this true for you? If so, how would you like your religion to be and more pure and faultless?

Incomplete Obedience: Doing Almost All of God's Will

1 Samuel 15:1-23

Perhaps one of the cleverest schemes of the enemy is to convince us that doing most of God's will is enough, and that by doing it we will receive God's blessings. King Saul fell into such a temptation. Saul was on a downward slide and accelerating as he neared the bottom. No matter what he was given to do, he came short of complete obedience. In this chapter, he was commanded and instructed by God to fight and destroy the Amalekites, the nation that had mercilessly ambushed the Hebrew stragglers when they had left Egypt on the way to Canaan. The order was very clear, everything that breathed was to be destroyed; it was devoted to God. For God's longsuffering had put up with the people of Amalek for years, but his word against them had not changed. They were to be blotted out as punishment for their sins. Instead of Saul following God's instructions, he succumbed to the wishes of his fighting men and did only part of God's command. Saul was never short of excuses for he was always constantly redefining the Lord's commands, doing what seemed best to him, rather than what God said. But to obey is better than sacrifice and because he rejected the word of the Lord, he was rejected as king. Obedience first, last, and always. We should not allow pressure from people around us to have a greater influence on our life than God.

Focus Scripture: 1 Samuel 15:1-23

"Wherefore then didst thou not obey the voice of the Lord, but didst fly upon the spoil, and didst evil in the sight of the Lord."

Focus Questions:

Are you constantly redefying the Lord's commands, doing what seems best to you rather than what God said is best? How does the scriptural description of King Saul's disobedience differ from the way you view your sins when you do not obey all of God's commands for our lives?

Meditation Points to Ponder:

Take a moment and think about an area in your life where you have been content to do almost all of God's will. Then ask yourself, what steps should I take to complete my obedience to God? For we must not allow pressure from the people around us to have greater influence on our life than God does.

The Consequences of Unbelief

Genesis 20:1-18

Have you ever gotten into trouble because you did not trust God to take care of you? Did you take matters into your own hands and in the process cut some moral and ethical corners? If so, you have company. It seems incredible to us that Abraham would again try to pass off Sarah as his sister within twenty years of the same blunder with Pharaoh. Why did he make the same mistake twice? Why should God's choice representative error in such a way, such a way to give a pagan king opportunity for a well-deserved rebuke. You see even Abraham through fear and temporary faithlessness (unbelief) resorted to a falsehood, deceit, and outright misrepresentation. He gave in to his fears and failed to tell the truth in a potentially dangerous situation. The Bible has no plaster saints. It doesn't cover over the sins of its heroes. So, we can learn from their failures as well as their successes.

In previous chapters, we saw Abraham at his best as he showed concern for a sinful city. In this chapter we find him <u>near</u> his worse as he pursues an immoral and unethical course of action that was potentially disastrous for everyone concerned. He told an untruth instead of relying on his belief in God, for God to work things out. It is shameful when a believer has to be justly rebuked by a man of word. When a half-truth is presented as the whole truth, it is untruth. But he will pay the consequence for his unbelief.

Abraham even tried to shift some of the blame onto God for making him wander in the first place. He would have been wiser to humbly acknowledge his guilt. Nevertheless, he was still God's man and so the Lord sent Abimelech to him so that Abraham would pray that his household be healed of its barrenness.

Focus Scripture: Genesis 20:2

"And Abraham said of Sarah his wife, she is my sister: and Abimelech King of Gerar sent and took Sarah."

Focus Question:

Take a moment and think of a difficult situation in which fear or unbelief led you to a course of action that was an untruth and its dishonor of god. What were the consequences and lessons you learned from it? How did you go about correcting that situation?

Meditation Point to Ponder:

Review the scriptures and determine how can Sarah and Abraham's experience encourage us to be more patient and faithful in waiting on god for unanswered prayer? What things in life have you struggled with recently? Tell God about them and allow him to take it from you as you come near to him in scripture.

Will You Be My Witness?

Acts 1:1-14

A story is told of a young man who told his friend, "If I were dying, what would I want most. I would be confidence that all I had believed about Jesus was true. I would want you to read scripture to me, pray with me, and talk to me about Jesus and heaven. The more I think about it, this confidence is what I needed not only when I am dying, but also when I am living. During the days between his resurrection and ascension, Jesus built the confidence of his disciples. He demonstrated and spoke truth about himself and then with a clearly defined task and the promise of the power to carry out the task. Having suppressed their curiosity as to the future date of this kingdom, the Lord Jesus directed their attention to what was more immediate, the nature and sphere of their mission. As to its nature, they were to be witnesses, as to its sphere, they were to witness in Jerusalem, and in all Judea, and Samaria, and to the end of the earth but first they must receive the power of the Holy Spirit. This power is indispensable of Christian witness. A person can be highly talented intensively trained and widely experienced but without spiritual power he is ineffective. On the other hand, a person may be uneducated, unattractive, and unrefined, yet let him be endued with the power of the Holy Spirit, and the world will turn out to see him for God the fearful disciple needed power for witnessing, they needed holy boldness for preaching the gospel. They would receive this power when the Holy Spirit came upon them. You are to be his witness, be confident that you can carry the message for that is your mission.

Focus Scripture: Acts 1:8

"But you shall receive power after the Holy Spirit is come upon you; and you shall be witnesses unto both in Jerusalem, and in all Judea, and Samaria, and unto the uttermost parts of the earth."

Focus Question:

For a moment, place yourself in the position of the Apostles. How would you feel if you were the first to be given the task described in verse eight? Briefly explain how are we equipped to handle the task assigned to us in verse eight?

Meditation Points to Ponder:

Take a moment and think about a time when your faith in Christ Jesus was encouraged by the words of others? Was your hope and confidence in Jesus affected by what you learned about him in this scripture? If so, how? Then thank God for giving you a task to carry out and tell him about the fears and joys you feel as his servant.

Your Struggle with Sin

Romans 7:7-25

Are you a Christian baffled by your behavior? You know the right thing to do, but you fail to do it. You resolve to avoid certain things, and they become even more attractive and enticing. Why? What keeps us from translating our desires into actions? In this scripture Paul explores his own struggles to do good and avoid evil. As we look into his mind and heart, we see a reflection of ourselves and the power that opposes us. You see, Paul emphasizes that the law itself is not sinful, but that it reveals sin in man. It was the law that convicted him of terrible depravity of his heart. For as long as he compared himself with other people, he felt fairly respectable, but as soon as the demand of God's law came home to him in convicting power, he stood speechless and condemned. For example, the one commandment that revealed sin to him was the tenth, I shall not covet. Coveting takes place in the mind. Although Paul not having committed any of the grosser, more revolting sins, he now realized that his rough life was corrupt. He understood that evil thoughts are sinful as well as evil deed. His outward life may have been relatively blameless, but his inward life was a chamber of horrors. Saying no to a T-bone steak we don't need seems so simple, but it is easier said than done. For sin takes opportunity by commandment but produces in us all manner of evil. "So, when I desire to do good, evil is always near." Therefore, we have come to realize that whenever an act is forbidden, the fallen nature wants to do it all the more. For example, "Stolen water is sweet, and bread eaten in secret is pleasant," apart from the law sin is dead relatively speaking. The sinful nature is like a sleeping dog. When the law comes and says, "Don't," the dog wakes up and goes on a rampage, doing excessively whatever is forbidden. But when the commandment came his sinful nature became inflamed. The more he tried to obey, the worse he failed.

Focus Scripture: Romans 7:8-9

"But sin, taking occasion by the commandment, wrought in me all manner of coveting, except the law had said, thou shalt not covet. For I was alive apart from the law once; but when the commandment came, sin revived, and I died."

Focus Question:

The law created in Paul a vivid awareness of sin, how? Why would it be wrong to blame the law for Paul's spiritual death? In verses 14-20, Paul feels so wretched, why is this?

Meditation Points to Ponder:

Saying no thank you to a T-bone steak that we do not need appears to be so simple and easy, however, it is easier said than done. Have you recently struggled to do what you know you should have done? Paul had many struggles in these verses. To what extent can you identify with his struggles? It is important to realize that only Christ can rescue you from the power of sin. Why is this important to know?

Knowing Our Advent Themes

1 Peter 1:3-5, 13-21

I believe that all scripture is somehow related, and all scripture is relevant. Nevertheless, I was surprised when the November reading in the book of Peter touched on all four themes of advent, that period of time on the church calendar when many Christians prepare to celebrate the first coming of Christ while looking forward to his second coming. Doing advent, we emphasize hope, peace, joy, and love, which God sent with Christ.

- **"Hope:** We have an inheritance reserved in heaven, a living hope through the resurrection of Christ from the dead (1 Peter 1:3-5).
- **Peace:** We will love life and see good days if we turn from evil and do good and if we seek peace, for peace comes from accepting Christ as your Savior, for the Lord watched over the righteous and hears their prayers. (1 Peter 3:10-12).

- **Joy:** We have inexpressible joy even though we have trials, tribulations, because our faith is being tested and proven genuine. The end of this faith is the salvation of our souls (1:6-9)
- **Love:** We can love one another with a pure heart because we have been born again through the word of God which lives and abides forever (1:22-23) because Christ came the first time, we can live with hope, peace, joy, and love till he comes again."

Remember the hope we have is in Jesus Christ, for it is he who brings joy into our hearts, and when we know him, the love of God, his peace will impart if you are looking for hope, peace, joy, and love this Christmas season, look to God, in him you will find it.

Focus Scripture: 1 Peter 1:3-5, 13-21

"Blessed be the God and Father of our Lord Jesus Christ, which according to his abundant mercy hath begotten us again unto a lively hope by the resurrection of Jesus Christ from the dead."

Focus Question:

Study Peter's description of the people who were about to receive this letter (1-2). How does his description of them help explain why they were strangers in the world?

Meditation Points to Ponder:

Hope, peace, joy, and love God sent with his son Jesus Christ, how does these attributes described here help you or offer you hope in your own setting? When have you seen Jesus, through a person or event in a way that has increased your faith?

Thanksgiving Pardon Fellowship and Forgiveness

1 John 1:1-10

Each year prior to the end of November, the President of the United States issues an official pardon for the National Thanksgiving Turkey. During this lighthearted ceremony, one president remarked: "Our guest of honor looks a little nervous. Nobody's told him yet that I'm going to give him a pardon." The poor turkey had a reason to be uneasy, because without an acquittal, he was doomed to be Thanksgiving dinner.

We as individuals are in similar situations when it comes to our sin for the word says "The blood of Jesus Christ, God's son cleanses us from our sin." Therefore, without God's pardon we are on our way to certain demise. This condition is a direct result of our wrongdoing. The bible says, "The wages of sin is death." However, we can be set free from this death sentence because God's son bore our sins in his body on the cross, "That we, having died to sin, might live for righteousness, by whose stripes you were healed." First John 1:7 tells us, "That Jesus' blood cleanses us from all our sins." Therefore, all God's forgiveness is based on the blood of his son that was shed at Calvary. That blood provided God with a righteous basis on which he can forgive sins so we can accent God's pardon for our sins and receive eternal life when we confess that Jesus Christ is Lord and believe that God has raised him from the dead. So, through faith in Christ, we receive God's pardon and escape sin's penalty. When we do that, we can claim the promise that God is faithful in the sense that he has promised to forgive and will abide by his promise. He is just to forgive because he has found a righteous basis for forgiveness in the substitutionary work of the Lord Jesus on the cross. Not only does he guarantee to forgive, but also to cleanse us from all unrighteousness.

I ask you today to consider how you will respond to God's offer of forgiveness. "For great is thy faithfulness," pardon for sin and a peace that endureth thine own dear presence to cheer and to guide: strength for today and bright hope for tomorrow, blessings all mine with ten thousand beside. For great is they faithfulness Lord unto me."

Focus Scripture: 1 John 1:1-10

"But if we walk in the light as he is the light, we have fellowship one with another and the blood of Jesus Christ his son cleanse us from all sin."

Focus Question:

John begins this chapter by announcing an apostolic message. What is the content of that message and what are John's reasons for announcing his message? John provides a test by which we can know if we have fellowship with God, based on your study of this passage, what does it mean to have fellowship with God and each other?

Meditation Points to Ponder:

Does John's test strengthen or weaken your assurance as a believer of fellowship with God. Briefly explain how can we enjoy a greater fellowship with those who know the Father and the Son?

The Time is Now to Worship Him

Luke 2:8-20

We begin our worship service out the first Sunday of advent with a song of praise called "Come and Worship." You might have been expecting to hear one of the old Christmas carols. But after reading Luke's account of Jesus' birth, I noticed that the first Christmas did not have all of our modern-day parties, gifts, presents, and feasts, but it did include worship. Therefore, worship is a lifestyle of enjoying God, loving him and giving ourselves to be used for his purposes. There were several things we need to notice about the birth of Christ: first was that the news of this unique birth was not given to religious leaders in Jerusalem, but to the lowly Shepherds on Judean Hillsides, humble men who were faithful in their work. This has meaning for God chose very ordinary people, busy about very ordinary tasks, whose eyes first saw the glory of the coming of the Lord (Luke 2:9-11). An angel of the Lord came to the Shepherds, and a bright, glorious light shined all around them. Then the angel comforted them and broke the good news. It was good tidings of great joy for all the people. That very day, in nearby Bethlehem, a baby had been born. This baby was a Savior, who is Christ the Lord, which is expressed in his name Jesus; he is also Christ, the anointed of God the Messiah of Israel. Then he is Lord. God manifested in the flesh (Luke 2:12). How would the Shepherds recognize him? The angels have them a two-fold sign. First, the baby would be wrapped in swaddling clothes. They had seen babies wrapped in swaddling clothes before, but the angel had just announced that this baby was the Lord. No one had ever seen the Lord. No one had ever seen the Lord as a little baby wrapped in swaddling clothes. The second part of the sign was that he would be lying in a manger. It is doubtful that the shepherds had ever seen a baby in such an unlike place. This indignity was reserved for the Lord of life and glory when he came into our world. It makes our minds dizzy to think of the creator and sustainer of the universe entering human history not as a conquering military hero, but as a little baby, yet this is the truth of the incarnation. Worship him.

Focus Scripture: Luke 2:8-20

"And she brought forth her first-born son, and wrapped him in swaddling clothes, and laid him in a manger; because there was no room for them in the inn."

Focus Questions:

Luke gives the reader very few details of Jesus' birth, but what impression does he leave with you? For you what is most meaningful about Christmas? We like shepherds on our Christmas cards, however in those days they were considered as an outcast group. So, what is the angel's message would be incredible to them?

Meditation Points to Ponder:

As with other strategic events, Luke gives the historical setting of the birth of Christ, what implications does this setting suggest about the world into which Jesus came? How are Simeon and Anna's prophetic messages about Jesus similar yet they are different?

Miraculous Escape

Acts 16:19-31

Miracles are woven throughout the narrative of the Book of Acts. It is true that Jesus Christ is the same yesterday, today, and forever. His power is the same. He can still perform any kind of miracles. You see our lives should be changed with supernatural power. We should be constantly seeing God's hand in the marvelous converging of circumstances. We should be experiencing events in our lives that lie beyond the laws of probability. We should be aware that God is arranging contacts, opening doors, overruling opposition; our service should crackle with the supernatural.

We should be seeing direct answers to prayer. When our lives touch other lives, we should see something happening for God. We should see his hand in breakdowns, delays, accidents, losses, and seeming tragedies. We should experience extraordinary deliverances and be aware of strength, courage, peace, and wisdom beyond our natural limits. For God is still in the miracle business. If our lives are lived only on the natural level, how are we any different from non-Christians? God's will is that our lives should be supernatural, that the life of Jesus Christ should flow through us. When this takes place, impossibilities will melt, closed doors will open and power will surge. Then we will be supercharged with the Holy Spirit and the mind of Christ and when we get close to people, they will know and feel that we are people of God. In this text Satan was defeated as Paul and Silas at midnight prayed and sing praises unto God and brought about a miracle. Some of you are facing midnight. Sing and pray.

Focus Scripture: Acts 16:19-31

"And at midnight Paul and Silas prayed and sang praises unto God: and the prisoners heard them. And suddenly there was a great earthquake, so that the foundation of the prison was shaken: and immediately all the doors were opened, and everyone's bands were loosen."

Focus Question:

The slave owners had Paul and Silas jailed, their response to being in jail and being beaten was to pray and sing hymns. What would or how would you have reacted to that? Describe the events that led up to the jailers. Question: "What must I do to be saved?"

Meditation Points to Ponder:

How does your response to opposition to and suffering for the gospel compare and contrast to that of Paul and Silas? Paul and

Silas speak the truth of the gospel as well as living it out. How do you give both a verbal and a living witness to Jesus? Is there a person or task to which God is calling you? If so, what steps do you need to take for immediate and unreserved obedience?

Ten Keys to God's Character

Exodus 20:1-17

The most convincing orders are those issued in simple words. Stop-go, yes-no. There is no misunderstanding them. We who have been in military know that in military training, soldiers learn split-second obedience to concise commands. Their survival depends on it. In this scripture, we find God speaks ten words, the most majestic, moral commands ever spoken, and the clearest rules for humanity's welfare. They are the foundations of personal and national life. We must remember that the Ten Commandments, laws were not given as a means of salvation. It was given to a people already saved, in order to instruct them in the will of the Lord, so that they might fulfill God's purpose for them as a kingdom of priests and a holy nation. The revelation was given not to give life but to guide life. These laws also reveal God's character, and in this passage, Israel learns that God is much more than the God of food, water, military victories and natural calamities. The laws were to keep us and grow us closer to God in our walk with him as we are obedient to him. Ask yourself the question: What part, if any, have the Ten Commandments had in forming your faith, as we review them for you. Ask yourself the question, am I following God's law in my life? Remember these laws are for the saved.

1. "You shall have no other Gods but me.
2. You shall not make for yourself any idol, nor bow down to it or worship it.
3. You shall not misuse the name of the Lord your God.
4. You shall remember and keep the Sabbath day holy.
5. Respect your father and mother.
6. You must not commit murder.
7. You must not commit adultery.
8. You must not steal.
9. You must not give false evidence against your neighbor.
10. You must not be envious of your neighbor's goods. You shall not be envious of his house nor his wife, nor anything that belongs to your neighbor.

Focus Scripture: Exodus 20:1-117

"And God spake all these words, saying, I am the LORD thy God, which have brought thee out of the land of Egypt, out of the house of bondage. Thou shalt have no other gods before me."

Focus Questions:

What right did God have to issue these commands? What reason does he give for prohibiting idolatry? How would you interpret the promise given to those who honor their parents? Think of other ways in conveying not only a wrong against our neighbor but also against God?

Meditation Points to Ponder:

Spend time in meditation on how other gods or idols in our life compete for our allegiance? Reflect on all of the commandments, and then ask yourself the question: Am I following these commands as God has directed me to do? Where do you need to improve and on which commandments?

Obtaining the Peace of the Lord

Psalm 37:1-17

A story is told of a young man named Sam who was out for a Sunday afternoon on his bicycle. Coming to a narrow spot in the road he got off and walked his bike. He had only gone a short distance when a fast-moving car swerved toward him, forcing him to dive for the ditch. As the car drove off, he was filled with indignation and rage. What the driver did was foolish, but he was surprised at the intensity of his fuming response, for he wanted to yell, and shake his fist. Something was out of place with his spirit. In his quiet time, he discovered a list of unresolved hurts, wounds, and unforgiving grudges that he had never dealt with like David and did not enjoy the peace of God. "We must trust in the Lord, delight in the Lord commit your way to the Lord rest in the Lord and wait patiently for him." Refrain from anger and turn from wrath, if we want true peace, you see David had suffered plenty at the hands of the ungodly, unscrupulous men during his lifetime. In this Psalm he gives us advice on how to act when we become victims of wicked schemes and venomous tongues. "First, we must not allow ourselves not to fret because of evil doers. Our fretting is only hurting no one but ourselves and we are accomplishing nothing. Whatever else we do; we must not be envious of the unrighteous. This earth is the only Heaven they are ever going to have. Don't be agitated over them, just trust in the Lord and do good which means to rely on the God who punishes the ungodly, don't you do it. Rejoice and delight in the Lord, and he has promised to give you the desires of your heart. Commit your way to him and he shall bring it to pass; wait patiently on him." If you are to have true peace, for God is the one who brings that kind of peace, for it is he who gives to us the happy state of the godly and the short-lived prosperity of the wicked. Just trust God; he shall bring it to pass.

Focus Scripture: Psalm 37:1-17

"Fret not thyself because of evildoers, neither be thou envious against the workers of iniquity. For they shall soon be cut down like the grass, and wither as the green herb. Trust in the LORD, and do good; so shalt thou dwell in the land, and verily thou shalt be fed." (Verses 1-3)

Focus Questions:

David gives an unusually extensive list of exhortations to us in verses 1-7, list them in your own words and then determine what benefits God give to those who live this way? We are not to worry when those who are evil and they still succeed, why? Explain what the constraints between the righteous and the wicked are.

Meditation Points to Ponder:

The Psalmist David encourages you to delight in the Lord, what do you find delightful about knowing God? What hesitation do you have that would keep you from delighting in God? The first step in receiving God's peace is to stop shouting so loud, put down your burdens, then give them to God, why?

The Mercies of the Lord As We Have Hope In the Midst of Suffering

Lamentations 3:19-33

Hope is such an elusive quality. It is easy to be hopeful when life is going well. But it is harder to hang on to hope whenever trouble obscures our focus, in the midst of horrible suffering, however, the author of Lamentations learned how to experience hope when everything seemed hopeless. With a prayer to god to remember his bitter plight, yet with lingering depression, over his misery the prophet gets his eyes off himself and onto the Lord. Hope is revived when he remembers that the Lords mercies and compassions are new every morning and that his faithfulness is great. (21-24) He begins to cite lessons learned in the school of affliction. "It is good to wait quietly for the Lord's deliverance and to submit to his yoke early in life, for his yoke is easy and his burdens are light: he learned to accept divine chastening and human blow and insults without talking back (28-30). He learned that God's rejection is neither final nor causeless; his compassion and mercies will always follow (31-33). He learned that the Lord does not approve of oppression, injustice, or the denial of rights (34-36). He learned that God is sovereign, his word prevails, all things, serve his will, so to complain when he punishes sin is senseless." So, the way of the blessing is through self-examination, turning back to God with your hope placed in Christ Jesus. So, as we approach this Christmas, remember that Jesus is the reason we celebrate, and we should continue to place our hope in him that is the only hope we have.

Focus Scripture: Lamentations 3:19-21

"Remembering mine affliction and my misery, the wormwood and the gall. My soul hath them still in remembrance and is humbled in me. This I recall to my mind, therefore have I hope."

Focus Questions:

Why did the author feel so hopeless and why did his helplessness turn to hope? What did he remember about God that changed his perspective on suffering? What did you learn in this chapter about the relationship between God's judgment and his love?

Meditation Points to Ponder:

In what ways had God been faithful to you? One way to deal with hopelessness is to be reminded of the character of God. How can you get to know God better?

God's Comfort for His People

Isaiah 43:1-13

"But now thus saith the Lord that created thee O Jacob, and he that formed thee O Israel fear not, for I have redeemed thee, I have called thee by thy name, thou art mine." How do you feel when you hear the words, I love you? We should not be ashamed to express these feelings, but many of us have never, or seldom, heard these words. Sometimes, like a radio signal cluttered with static the true meaning of the words is distorted by their overuse in countless songs, books, and movies. In this passage of scripture, we will hear these words afresh so that we can be made abundantly sure of God's love for us personally. In tones of tender love, God assures his people that they need not fear, because he who created, formed, redeemed, and called them will be with them in the flood and fire. The holy one of Israel gives Egypt as their ransom, a promise that was fulfilled after the return of the Jews from captivity.

Because Israel is precious, honored, and loved, God will give men in exchange for her that his judgment will fall on the gentiles in every direction in order that his sons and his daughters might be restored to the land. For the Lord calls Israel as his witnesses, they should testify that he is the only true God, that he is eternal, that besides him there is no Savior and Deliverer and that his decrees and acts cannot be thwarted. For he is our Savior and he loves us.

Focus Scripture: Isaiah 43:1-13

"Since thou wast precious in my sight, thou hast been honorable, and I have loved thee: therefore, will I give men for thee, and people for thy life. Fear not: for I am with thee: I will bring thy seed from the east, and gather thee from the west."

Focus Questions:

Israel is called to an international assembly of idol-worshipers and their idols in verses 8-13. To what does the Lord call Israel to witness to? We see that Israel's slavish religiosity which does not please God. What promise does he repeat to his people and why?

Meditation Points to Ponder:

How do you feel about being the object of the loving statement? God is the one who bring into existence things into our lives that did not exist. What new things do you need to look with expectant faith, for God to do for you that will transform your life?

Knowing and Doing God's Will

Ephesians 5:17-21

A young man facing the future and unsure of what the next, day, month, or year would bring, concluded, "That nobody knows what God's will is." Is he right? Does a lack of certainty about the future translate into not knowing god's will? Well the concept of knowing God's will is often limited to discerning what specific situation we will be in at some future time. Although we seek God's specific leading is part of it, another aspect that is just as vital is to follow the clearly defined elements of God's will each and every day. For instance, "If it is God's will for us to be good citizens as a challenge to those opposed to Christ (1 Peter 2:15) to give God thanks no matter what (1 Thess 5:18) (Give thanks in all circumstances, for this is God's will for you in Christ Jesus. To be sanctified sexually, avoiding immorality (1 Thess. 4:3) for it is God's will that you should be sanctified, that you should avoid sexual immorality and learn to control your own body, to live under the Holy Spirit (Ephesians 5:18) to sing to him (v19) and to submit to God in these and other areas, we are more likely to live in what Romans 12:2 calls God's good and acceptable and perfect will." Living with God's smile of approval leads to his guidance for your future. As you seek to know God's will for the future, you must also act on what we already know, knowing God's will for the future, comes when we follow today what he has revealed in the scriptures as his commands to obey love and obey the Lord every day and he will unfold your future. So, we should not be unwise but we ought to understand what the will of the Lord is. This is a crucial matter, because of the abounding evil and the shortness of the time; we might be tempted to spend our days in frantic and feverish activity of our own choosing. But this would amount to nothing but wasted energy.

The most important of this is to find out God's will for us each day and do it. This is the only way to be efficient and effective. It is all too possible to carry on Christian work according to our own ideas and in our own strength, and be completely out of the will of the Lord. The path of wisdom is to discern God's will for our individual lives, then to obey it to the hilt.

Focus Scripture: Ephesians 5:17-18

"Wherefore be ye not unwise, but understanding what the will of the Lord is. And be not drunk with wine, wherein is excess; but be filled with the Spirit;"

Focus Questions:

Describe several beneficial results of being filled with the spirit and in our own words explain the characteristics of those who are filled with the spirit? What have you observed about God that you have begun or could begin to imitate and be in his will?

Meditation Points to Ponder:

Look again at the scripture. How could you use thanksgiving to replace improper behavior in your life? How could you live more wisely and be in the will of God?

Why Flee When You Can Trust?

Psalm 11:1-7

Psalm 11 is an antidote for gloomy headlines. When the news is all bad, wars, violence, crime, corruption, and political unrest, David reminds us that we can rise above the circumstances of life by keeping our eyes on the Lord. It seems that when David had opened his front door, a frenzied visitor burst in. His face was pale and drawn, his eyes were popping with excitement and his lips were quivering. In jerky, breathless gasps he told of imminent disaster and advised David to head for the hills. This Psalm is David's answer to the pessimistic visitor's counsel of despair and discouragement. David first states his simple trust in the Lord as his refuge. Why flee when you can trust God? Then he reproaches to calamity Charlie for seeking to disturb his peace. Notice that the text contains the words of the gloom peddler. He tells David to flee as a bird to your mountain, in fact he tells him that you are insignificant and defenseless as a little bird, the best thing you can do is escape because criminals have the upper hand ready to gun down decent citizens. What hope do you think there is for a righteous person like you? What hope? Why? The Lord of course. The Lord is in his holy temple and nothing can stop the fulfillment of his plans. Just as God hates the violent man, so he loves the righteous. The ultimate reward of the upright will be to stand in God's presences. So, we need not get all upset over the headlines. The waves of adverse circumstances may seem to be against us at any particular time but the tide of God's irresistible purpose is sure to win in the end, just trust God.

The poet puts it this way: "He everywhere hath sway, and all things serve his might: his every act pure blessing is, his path unsullied light.

We comprehend him not, yet earth and heaven tell, God sits as sovereign on the throne and ruleth all things well." (Author Unknown) So just rejoice in the providence and justice of God. Trust in the Lord. The writer declared, "Tis so sweet to trust in Jesus, just to take him at his word, just to rest upon his promise, just to know, thus saith the Lord! Jesus, Jesus, how I trust him! How I've proved him o'er and o'er. Jesus, Jesus, precious Jesus! Oh, for grace to trust him more!"

Focus Scripture: Psalm 11:1-2

"In the LORD put I my trust: how say ye to my soul, Flee as a bird to your mountain? For, lo, the wicked bend their bow, they make ready their arrow upon the string, that they may privily shoot at the upright in heart."

Focus Questions:

Can you recall a time when you felt helpless? Then picture God in that situation with you as your refuge, your protector, and defender. How does that make you feel? How does the writer describe God and his actions on behalf of people who have been abused?

Meditation Points to Ponder:

How would you like God to respond to your feelings of helplessness? What is God's attitude toward the wicked and what will happen to them in their attacks upon the righteous?

We Are Called to Be Different

1 Peter 1:13-25

I grew up in a church of fervent Christians. We knelt to pray, we carried our bibles, and we wore modest clothes to school and church, even to gym classes. We talked a lot about Jesus and his death upon the cross for our redemption. We talked about being saved and obedient to our parents. Needless to say, kids from our church never made the most popular list at the local high school. We were square and because we often shouted, we feared the Taunt Holy Roller, that's what they called us.

You need to know that it is possible that our attempts to be separate and holy did more to close people out of our belief than to invite them in. Yet, God has called his Christian people to be different, different from what they would be if they did not believe in Jesus. Jesus was different from the unbelievers around him and we should also be different. Well, in this scripture Peter gives us several exhortations:

1. Have a girded mind; gird up the loins of your mind. As believers, we are to avoid panic and distraction. A girded mind is one that is strong, composed, cool and ready for action. It is unimpeded by the distraction of human fear or persecution.

2. Be sober, self-controlled. A sober spirit is poised and stable, not one of hysteria.

3. Have an optimistic forward-looking mind, resting in God. Resting your hope fully upon the grace that is brought to you at the revelation of Jesus Christ.

4. Be obedient children not indulging in the sins you use to do. Now that you are Christians, we should pattern our lives after the one whose name we bear, Jesus Christ.

5. Instead of imitating the ungodly world with fads and fashion, our lives should reproduce the Holy character of God who called us. We must be Holy in all that we do because he is Holy, and we are called to be different. We are to be Christ like Christians. If we are to be like him, we must be holy in all that we do and say. In this life, we will never be as holy as he is, but we should be holy as he is, but we should be holy because he is.

Focus Scripture: 1 Peter 1:13-25

"But as he which called you is holy, so be ye holy in all manner of conversation; because it is written, be ye holy; for I am holy."

Focus Question:

Reflect for a moment and think about a devout Christian that you respect, admire, and love, then in what ways this person resembles Christ and his attributes?

Meditation Points to Ponder:

In this scripture Peter gives us several ways how followers of Jesus ought to respond to his gift of salvation. Take a movement and define each of them to your own understanding. Select one of them, and decide if this is your priority, what changes would you have to make in your life in order to be like Christ?

Examine Yourselves

2 Corinthians 13:1-11

I want to you to imagine life without a final examination. At first it strikes us as a wonderful vacation like school without test and report cards. But without accountability, life quickly loses its meaning. The whole bible looks toward the final day with vibrant hope. Those genuinely in Christ have nothing to fear and everything to anticipate and look forward to. But what of those who are not sure of their salvation? What about those who don't know that assurance of their salvation come first and foremost through the word of God? You see, the moment we trust Christ, we can know on the authority of the Bible that we have been born again. As times go on, we do find other evidence of the new life, a new love for holiness, a new hatred of sin, a love for the word and the brethren, practical, righteousness, obedience, and separation from the world. If we have these things, we will not have false confidence about the outcome of our final exam. So, look closely at yourself to see if you are living in the faith, test yourself, do you not realize that Christ Jesus is in you? Unless you fail the test. Make the necessary adjustments to keep your strong relationship with Christ. Then you will be just fine in your exam.

Focus Scripture: 2 Corinthians 13:1-11

"Whether ye be in the faith: prove your own selves. Know ye not your own selves, how Jesus Christ is in you, except ye be reprobates?"

Focus Questions:

Paul asks them to examine themselves not so much in their doctrine as in their experience. How could the Corinthians know experientially that they truly belonged to Christ? In what ways does Paul show that he cares more for their passing the test in the eyes of others? In what specific ways does Paul pray they will be built up?

Meditation Points to Ponder:

In what way do you shrink from your daily cross and find your power elsewhere? If you are unsure of your position in Christ, what can you do about it in light of what you have read in this chapter?

Stand Firm (Fast) in the Lord

Philippians 4:1-9

Take a moment to think of the people you love, admire, respect, and care about the most in your life. What is your greatest desire for these people? On the basis of the wonderful hope which the apostle had set before the minds of the believers in the previous verse. He now exhorts them to stand fast in the Lord. Paul thinks of the Philippians; his greatest desire is that they will stand firm in what they have been taught. But he was also aware of some problems which may cause their faith to weaken. Remember that we will always experience some types of problems and difficulties which will have tendency to weaken our faith life. That is the time to really stay firm to your convictions, hold on to what you believe and to trust only in God. Paul writes to them that in order to stand firm they must put an end to disagreements, rejoice always in the Lord. Fill your thoughts with good things. Hold on to God's unchanging hand as you stand for that which is right. As the word says, "Therefore my beloved brethren, be yet steadfast, unmovable, always abounding in the work of the Lord. For as much as ye know that your labor is not in vain in the Lord." (1 Co. 15:58) Stay close to the Lord and remain steadfast in the Lord, and in all that you do. Eventually, you will come out alright if you will remain faithful, in spite of problems, difficulties, and oppositions. We must realize that it is possible as far as things of the Lord are concerned. For us to submerge our petty, personal differences in order that the Lord may be magnified, and his work is advanced. Therefore, stand fast in what you have been taught, in what you believe, knowing that God will see you through, even if you have to stand alone. Stand fast, firm, and resolute in your convictions.

Focus Scripture: Philippians 4:1-2

"Therefore, my brethren dearly beloved and longed for, my joy and crown, so stand fast in the Lord, my dearly beloved. I beseech Euodias, and beseech Syntyche, that they be of the same mind in the Lord."

Focus Question:

This chapter opens with a statement for us to stand firm in the Lord, how then can we stand firm in the Lord, and how can each of the promises and command in verses 4-7 help you to be joyful, peaceful and free of anxiety?

Meditation Points to Ponder:

We should have a response to disagreements within the church, what should be our responses? The word tells us that the God of peace will be with us as we practice what we have learned. What principles have you learned that you need to put into practice so that your thoughts and attitudes will not be robbed of you and your faith will not be weakened?

Facing Temptation: David's Fall

2 Samuel 11:1-26

A story is told of a pastor who every year would faithfully deliver a message on the evils of birth control. His sermon was entitled, "If you didn't want to go to Chicago, why did you get on the train." His point of course was that if we want to avoid certain consequences, we must avoid certain actions. In other words, we must face temptation daily and know how to handle each one of them. In this scripture we find David's notorious moral lapse was occasioned by three things: 1. His neglect of his own business, 2. Love of ease and the indulgence of a slothful temper; 3. A wandering eye. You need to realize that sin often begins with a series of temptations, each one leading to the next, until at some point that temptation becomes a sin that must be recognized and dealt with. The story of David and Bathsheba reveals how a series of smaller sins can build into tragic and devastating results. We also discover from reading of this scripture the forces that can lead a man after God's own heart to commit adultery and murder. The scripture reports this incident from the life of David is an indicator of their faithfulness. It gives us an honest and uncut view of God's people the way they really were. Remember to shun the very appearance of evil, and do not yield to temptation, for God will see you through.

Focus Scripture: 2 Samuel 11:2-5

"And it came to pass in an eveningtide, that David arose from off his bed, and walked upon the roof of the king's house: and from the roof he saw a woman washing herself; and the woman was very beautiful to look upon. And David sent and enquired after the woman. And one said, is this not Bathsheba, the daughter of Eliam, the wife of Uriah the Hittite? And David sent messengers and took her; and she came in unto him, and he lay with her; for she was purified from her uncleanness; and she returned unto her house. And the woman conceived, and sent and told David, and said, I am with child."

Focus Question:

Sin often begins with a series of temptations, each one of them leading to the next. What steps led to David's sin with Bathsheba? At each stage of his temptation, he had an opportunity to stop. What could David have done to keep from taking the next step?

Meditation Points to Ponder:

From this chapter, how would you explain what led "a man after God's own heart" to commit adultery and murder? Why are we tempted to cover up our sins rather than confess them? Finally, in what specific way is David's experience a warning to you?

Confession and Forgiveness

Psalm 32:1-11

Just as cholesterol is the silent killer of the physical heart, guilt, and unforgiveness is the silent killer of our souls. Cholesterol accumulates slowly over the years, and then residue left by a poor diet, inadequate exercise or other sins, guilt, accumulates, perhaps genetic malfunctions. So, it is with unforgiveness/guilt. Little by little, with each act of envy, with each thought of a bad experience, with hurt, lust, anger, resentment or other sin, this stuff (guilt and unforgiveness) accumulates around the human heart and begins to affect our spiritual walk with the Lord. Even though we are believers we cannot find happiness, or peace of mind for the burden of unforgiveness (guilt) is still there. But today I bring you this good news, and that is God won't let us succumb to guilt without many warnings the exposure of guilt is not for the purpose of condemnation (as it is with Satan) but for the cleansing our hearts and restoring the flow of his love. How can we say that we love God, if we are still hold unforgiveness against others? The cause of frustration for many people, or envious or resentfulness today is because of the lack of confusion and forgiveness. What you must do is to give your feelings over to God one by one and allow him to heal your wounded heart.

For happiness is to be forgiven. It is an emotion that defies description. It is the relief of an enormous burden lifted, of a debt that has been cancelled of a conscience at rest. For guilt is gone, the warfare is ended, and over, peace is enjoyed. To David it meant the forgiveness of his greatest transgression, the covering of his sin, the now-imputation of his iniquity, and the cleansing of his spirit from deceit. To the believer today it means more than the mere covering of his sin; for that was the Old Testament concept of atonement. However, in this age the believer knows that his sins have been put away completely and they have been buried forever in the sea of God's forgetfulness. For blessed is the man whose sins are forgiven.

Focus Scripture: Psalm 32:1-2, 5

"Blessed is he whose transgression is forgiven, whose sin is covered. Blessed is the man unto whom the LORD imputeth not iniquity, and in whose spirit there is no guile...I acknowledge my sin unto thee, and mine iniquity have I not hid. I said, I will confess my transgressions unto the LORD; and thou forgavest the iniquity of my sin."

Focus Questions:

It is interesting that David experienced a sense of protection after receiving forgiveness; but how might unconfessed sin have made him feel vulnerable and somewhat exposed? In verses 8-9 David records the Lord's promise of guidance. From these verses, what is the condition of receiving God's guidance?

Meditation Points to Ponder:

Consider now for a moment whether there are things in your past for which you are guilty but have never sought forgiveness? Name them and take time to confess them and ask for God's forgiveness. Are there things in your past for which you feel guilty but for which there was really no wrong done? Explain?

Is Faith Always Worthwhile?

Job 42:1-16

Today's scripture lesson begins with a question. Is faith always worthwhile? Is it money? Is it power? Is it success? Is it possessions of material things? Every Christian believer comes to these questions at some time or another in their walk with God. For it is, after all, Satan's questions in the first chapter of Job. So, the fateful test is designed, the test to see whether Job's faith is without any ulterior motive or as Satan's believes, merely a commercial contract rather than a covenant of belonging. You know the story how the Lord allowed Job his servant a perfect upright man for Satan to take all he had, caused him to lose his possessions, family, and then afflicted his body. His friends reasoned that God was punishing Job because of his sins, but that was not right; his wife advised Job to curse God and die. Yet through all of this, Job remained faithful unto God. So, in the end after Job prays for his friends, he has his fortune restored and is given a new family. The story ends with Job living happily ever after and dying old and full of years. But was Satan, right? Is unselfish faith right or even possible? How should we react when we hear someone talking about the benefits of following Jesus? Is faith really worthwhile? I believe so to the very end. Holding on to faith is the thing to do, to the end.

For as soon as Job prayed for them, the Lord restored in reverse order twice as much as Job had before: twice as many sheep, camels, oxen, and female donkeys. He also received seven sons and daughters, which doubled his family, since he presumably still had the first one in heaven. Job lived an additional one hundred and forty years, the Lord blessed the latter days of Job more than his beginning, so Job died old and full of days. In all of this, Job did not curse God as Satan said he would. It is lovely touches of God's grace that Job, who had been so hideously disfigured by his disease, after his restoration had daughters who were exceptionally beautiful. Job also gave them an inheritance with their brothers, probably not a common practice in the patriarchal era. So, yes it pays to be faithful.

Focus Scripture: Job 42:10, 12-13

10 "And the LORD turned the captivity of Job, when he prayed for his friends: also the LORD gave Job twice as much as he had before.

12 So the LORD blessed the latter end of Job more than his beginning: for he had 14 thousand sheep, and 6 thousand camels, and a thousand yoke of oxen, and a thousand she asses.

13 He had also 7 sons and 3 daughters."

Focus Questions:

How do you react when you hear someone talking about the benefits of following Jesus, when you have never received some of the blessings? The fateful test is designed to see whether Job's faith is without any ulterior motive or as Satan believes, merely a commercial contract rather than a covenant of belonging. Was Satan, right? Is unselfish faith possible or even desirable?

Meditation Points to Ponder:

In what sense may suffering Christians look forward to the blessings of God? What have you learned through this study about loving God for God's sake? What have you learned about him and the way he works in the world through the book of Job?

If I'm Living Right, Then Why Do I Hurt So Much?

1 Peter 3:8-22 KJV

We often assume that there is a direct connection between right living and easy living. We say I'm saved, I gave my life to the Lord, I am living right, and yet I still hurt. It is an added pat on the back when life runs smoothly. But it is an unspoken accusation when trauma strikes, when problems and difficulties come. Peter contemplated this connection, and warns us that sometimes suffering comes, whether or not we earn it. Our question might be why? The answer might be that God is trying to produce Christlikeness in each of his children. This process necessarily involves suffering, frustration, and perplexity. Not easy living. For the fruit of the spirit cannot be produced when all is sunshine, there must be rain and dark clouds. Trials never seem pleasant; they seem very difficult and disagreeable. But afterwards they yield the peaceable fruit of righteousness to those who are trained by them. Therefore, we should never become despondent or discouraged looking for easy living when passing through trials and difficulties of life, for no problems is too great for our Father. Some problems in life are never removed. We must learn to accept and to prove that his grace is sufficient. Paul asked the Lord three times to remove a physical infirmity; the Lord did not but gave him grace to bare it. When we face problems in life, know that Peter made no promise of easy living. Sometimes suffering comes whether or not we earn it. We must be submissive to the will of God. The gifted blind hymn writer wrote.

"What a happy soul am I, although I cannot see? I am resolved that in this world, contended I will be. How many blessings I enjoy that other people don't? To weep and sigh because I'm blind, I cannot and I won't." –Fannie Crosby

Therefore, the believer must have a good conscience, if he or she knows they are innocent of any crime, and then they can go through persecution of any kind with the boldness of a lion. But if we have a bad conscience, we will be plagued with feelings of guilt and will not be able to stand against the foes. Even if a believer's life is blameless, the enemies of the gospel will still find fault with them and bring false charges against you. But when the case comes to trial and the charges are found to be empty, the accusers will be ashamed. Sometimes Christians must suffer which might be God's will for us and it should be for doing good. But we should not bring suffering on ourselves for our misdeeds, for there is no virtue in that.

Focus Scripture: 1 Peter 3:14, 16-17 KJV

[14] "But and if ye suffer for righteousness' sake, happy are ye: and be not afraid of their terror, neither be troubled

[16] Having a good conscience; that, whereas they speak evil of you, as of evildoers, they may be ashamed that falsely accuse your good conversation in Christ.

[17] For it is better, if the will of God be so, that ye suffer for well doing, than for evil doing."

Focus Questions:

In spite of godly living, Peter knew that Christians may encounter suffering and hardship. What advice and counsel does Peter offer for coping with suffering? Why might the unbeliever be willing to listen to reasons for hope from a person who is living the way Peter describes?

Meditation Points to Ponder:

How could setting ourselves apart for Christ as Lord help us endure suffering? Our world is often unjust, call to your mind some of your past or current sufferings in the content of these sufferings how can the picture of Christ portrayed by this scripture bring you hope?

The Joy of Growing Up In Christ

Galatians 4:1-20

I believe that God wants us to grow up as believers. So that we can receive all the blessing that growth produces. But have you ever longed to be a child again, to be free from work, rent, mortgage payments, bill and taxes? Can you remember the carefree days, when from morning till night your job was to play or be entertained? The Galatians did. In this scripture Paul gives us the picture of a wealthy father who intends to turn over control of his wealth to the son when he reaches maturity. However, as long as he is still a child, the heir status is like that of a slave. He is continually told to do this and not to do that. He has stewards who manage his property and guardians in charge of his person. So, although the inheritance is surely his, he does not enter into it until he has grown up. This is where the Galatians and some of us are longing to return to the spiritual childhood of the law. But aren't we forgetting something?

Look at all the things we couldn't do as children. Look at all the blessing that he has brought to us on this Christian journey. So, you are no longer a slave, but a son and since you are a son, God has made you also an heir. So, when you did not know God, you were slaves to those who by nature are not God. But now that you know God, no one can enslave you. Therefore, grow-up in Christ and begin to obtain the blessing of God and start living the abundant life. For we must remember that Christ came to redeem mankind and to give both to Jews and Gentiles the adoption of sons. Therefore, we must grow in our relationship with the Lord, Jesus Christ. If we are to obtain the abundant life, and have life and have it more abundantly. We cannot remain spiritually immature and receive the blessing from the Lord.

Focus Scripture: Galatians 4:1-5

"Now I say, that the heir, as long as he is a child, differeth nothing from a servant, though he be lord of all; But is under tutors and governors until the time appointed of the father. Even so we, when we were children, were in bondage under the elements of the world: But when the fulness of the time was come, God sent forth his Son, made of a woman, made under the law, To redeem them that were under the law, that we might receive the adoption of sons."

Focus Questions:

How was life under the law like spiritual childhood? Yet when the time had fully come, God sent his son, how did things change because of his coming? How do verses 12-20 illustrate the care and concern we should have for other members of God's family?

Meditation Points to Ponder:

Think about in what ways do you sometimes act like a spiritual slave? How can you begin to act more like God's beloved son or daughter? Spend a few minutes each day of intimate prayer with the Father, thanking him for the privilege of being a member of his family.

God's Way or No Way

Rev. Dr. Freddie A. Banks, Jr.

I Corinthians 2:9-10 KJV

"But as it is written, eye hath not seen, nor ear heard, neither have entered into the heart of man, the things which God hath prepared for them that love him."

"But God hath revealed them unto us by His spirit: for the Spirit searcheth all things, yea, the deep things of God."

Today I want to focus mainly on two Bible characters and the scripture text, I Corinthians 2:9-10 to paraphrase it, no eye has seen, no ear has heard, no mind has conceived what God has planned for you or me, if I do things his way. Having worked with young people for a number of years who are trying to succeed in a world filled with opposition, I know how difficult it is for you to keep going strong when others try to hinder you. I know what it means to be around people who are complacent, and are not attempting to better their lives and are going absolutely nowhere, and no place. They make fun of you because you have a desire to be more than you are. Being in an environment like this can often cause Christians to question themselves. Do I really want to do this? Is this really worth it? Can I even accomplish it? The problem begins when these questions pop into our minds. My purpose today, and throughout my educational and ministerial career has been to encourage people to become all that God has intended them to be in their lives. By using their God given potential, and despite outside influences, circumstances, and conditions, never doubt themselves, but to always lean on the Lord for what they want, need, and desire.

There are 3 principles that I believe you must do in order to obtain that which God has planned for you. My prayer is that you will take mental and written note of these. As you keep them in your mind and heart, so that everyday new doors will open for you and your life will flourish.

1. The first principle you must apply to your life is that of never doubting yourself or God. For the word of God says, "For verily I say unto you that whosoever shall say to the mountain, be removed, and be thou cast into the seal'; and shall not doubt in his heart, but shall believe that those things which he saith shall come to pass; he shall have whatsoever he said." (Mark 11:23) Let me use a well-known Bible character to get this principle across to you. We are all familiar with Moses and the burning bush. God called Moses to do great things. But what did Moses do? He began to complain about the dangers of the task God

gave him. He began to worry about his image, he doubted his own ability to take the assignment and evoke change and then he had the nerve to doubt that God could change the mind of Pharaoh and let the Israelites go. We can be just like Moses. Uncertain, afraid, skeptical. We have the desire to do great things, but we lack the proper will. Moses was afraid that the Egyptians would kill him. We have a tendency to worry that when we get out in the world trying to achieve our goals that people will not like us. Like Moses, fearful of what his friends, family, and associates would think about him. But this is a big mistake on our part. Because if you are doing what God wats you to do, it doesn't matter what people think and if they are opposed to your accomplishments maybe they were not your true friends anyhow.

Moses had a speech impediment that he worried would prohibit him from doing what God waned him to do. He says to God, "God I can't go before Pharaoh, I don't speak to well, and I stumble over my words." Just another excuse. We do the same thing every day. You don't try out for the team because your right-hand lay-up is off. You won't apply for the job you want because you think you are not qualified, or you won't try out for the track team because you don't run the 4 x 1 as well as you should. The key here is to trust God and his plan for your life. Don't worry about whether or not people are going to like what you are about. Don't ask God if there is a better person, for clearly if he called you through his word or a prayer, he wants you, not someone else. You have to have faith enough to believe that if he has chosen you, he is going to provide a way for you to accomplish what he needs you to do. You won't get things done otherwise. Sure, Moses may have had his worries, and yes, Pharaoh denied his request for freedom ten times. But you better believe that Moses eventually led God's people out of Egypt and across the Red Sea while Pharaoh and his army perished. God moved his enemies, his haters and let him walk right through to freedom. All Moses had to do and all you have to do is stop doubting, trust him and have a little faith.

2. Secondly, just because you are a Christian, young or old one does not mean that you cannot be used by God to do great things. I have heard many times in my life from people, "I cannot do this or I cannot do that, because I am too little, or from adults: Wait until you get bigger or older. What you don't realize is that for children with dreams and desires, hearing those words can be discouraging. But do not get down on yourself because of your age or size. Take David for an example. God told Samuel that one of Jesse's sons was the new chosen King of Israel. David is the best example of a young person called to do a big person's job. God made Samuel bypass all 7 of Jesse's sons. He overlooked Usher and Omarion and went straight to Urkel. It doesn't matter that they were older, taller, bigger, and better looking. That is not what God looks for. I Samuel 16:7 says, "But the Lord said unto Samuel, look not on his countenance, or on the height of his stature, because

I have refused him: For the Lord seeth not as man seeth; for man looketh on the outward appearance but the Lord looketh at the heart." God wanted someone dedicated. He wants someone caring, someone who can lead and follow; someone who will trust him no matter the cost. He wants someone humble, someone like David, a child.

Well, you know the story as well as I do. David rose against Goliath, the leader of the Philistines. He ignored the negative vibes from Saul, his father, his brothers, and friends when they said he was too little. He paid them no mind and simply said, "If God delivered me from the paw of the lion. He will deliver me from the hand of this Philistine." Armed with only a sling-shot, a rock and his faith, David boldly faced Goliath. You know the ending of the story. Goliath was slain, and the Israelites defeated the Philistines. All the adults and soldiers, with their high and mighty attitudes, and their swords and shields, sat back as God worked a miracle through a young shepherd boy. Talk about something major for a small person. Hear me when I say that God has something for everyone right down to the youngest, smallest person in this sanctuary. You just have to be willing to let go and trust God, let God do the work.

Finally, I cannot say this enough, never stop believing in yourself, trusting in the Lord and loving God. This is something that will keep you in a right relationship with God. Try to remember that you are the righteousness of God, that you can do what the Bible says you can do. You receive by faith what the Bible says is rightfully yours based on your faith and your relationship with God. You will not walk in fear, guilt, condemnation or inferiority, but rather you will live and walk in holiness, authority, favor, and victory according to the word of God. My belief and faith in God, my love for the Lord is more than enough to override any and everything in opposition to me, and that is the way you should live in every aspect of your life. At school, at home, around your friends. The light of God should be shining in your life.

Always speak things that be as though they were. You must claim the things you want. Don't spend your time worrying about everyone else, and what they are doing. For this is your time to shine, stay in the will of God. You have to arm yourself with your will and the word of God. Forget about the haters, forget about the obstacles, forget about those who doubt you and focus on him who loves you, who has called you, prepared you, and be a determined soul, you can make it with God. **Remember it must be God's way, his will and not yours.**

The Institution of Marriage God's Plan for Marriage When One Plus One Equals One

Bride & Groom, has requested that we begin this solemn ceremony with a short message on the institution of marriage. I am very happy to adhere to their request. As this couple is very special to me, and it is my prayer that they live a long happy married life together. Genesis 2:21-25

This message is entitled: God's equation for marriage when one plus one equals one. The Bride & Groom, I would like for you to remember that God's plan for marriage involves four commitments that are lived out over a lifetime in the power of the Holy Spirit, and they are receiving, leaving, cleaving, and becoming one flesh.

Commitment number 1: receiving your mate in Genesis 2:21-25 we read, "So the God cause a deep sleep to fall upon the man, and he slept; then he took one of his ribs, and closed up the flesh at that place. And the Lord God fashioned into a woman the rib which he had taken from man, and brought her to man. And the man said, "This is bone of my bone, and flesh of my flesh: She shall be called woman, because she was taken out of man. Once God had made Adam, "A helper suitable for him (Genesis 2:18) one question remained: What would be Adam's response? If you will remember, He had been busy naming the animals when God used some celestial sominex to put him under rib surgery. No doubt, he had been dreaming of lions, tigers, and bears, yet now before him was God's custom-made helper. No Adam did not know anything about Eve except, she had come from God. So how did he respond?

"This is now bone of my bones and flesh of my flesh: she shall be called woman, for she was taken out of man." (Gen 2:23) The living Bible paraphrase comes closet to capturing the real spirit of Adam's response: "This is another way to interpret the exclamation is "Wow!" Where have you been all my life? In other words, Adam was excited-He was beside himself.

This passage illustrates a cornerstone principle of marriage. Just like Adam, both of you must individually receive your mate as God's provision for your need for companionship. You see receiving your mate demonstrates your faith in God's integrity.

For Adam's focus was on God's flawless character, not on Eve's performance. He knew God could be trusted. So, he enthusiastically received Eve, because he knew she was for him. Adam's faith in God enabled him to receive Eve as God's perfect provision for him.

As you enter in to this, marriage you must receive your mate in the same way that Adam received Eve. For you have decided that your fiancée's is indeed God's provision, you need to accept your fiancé and fiancée's strength and weakness. You must be willing to look beyond physical attractiveness to the God who is the provider, who knows what He is doing. Please be aware that receiving your mate is not just a decision you make when you recite your wedding vows. It requires an attitude, a continual acceptance throughout your marriage.

In the months and years after the wedding, each of you will become more and more aware of your responsibility to receive each other as God's provisions, as you become aware of your respective weakness and faults. The more you remember your responsibility to receive each other as God's provision, the stronger your marriage will become. For the person who knows you best also loves you the most, your marriage will truly be special.

Commitment number 2: Leave your parents.

Genesis 2:24, "For this cause a man shall leave his father and his mother and shall cleave to his wife; and they shall become one flesh."

As children, you were dependent upon your parents for the material and nonmaterial things in your lives. Your parents had the responsibility for providing food, shelter, and clothing, as well as emotional stability, godly values and spiritual growth. However, just as the doctor cuts the umbilical cord from the baby to the mother, so both of you must now cut the umbilical cord of dependency and allegiance to your parents. If you don't, you'll undermine the interdependence you are to build as husband and wife. You must sever the cord of dependency, which means, to rely on your parents for material and emotional support. You must also sever the cords of allegiance, yes, honor your parents, but your allegiance, your priority now become your spouse, your first and foremost loyalty is to God, and to each other. This act of breaking from one's parents, is absolutely fundamental to establishing oneness.

Commitment number 3: Cleave to your mate:

To cleave (Genesis 2:24) means to stick like glue. It is a permanent bond, not meant to be broken. Today, both of you will participate in one of the most solemn responsibilities ever given to humankind, ordained by God, the vows of marriage. This vow or covenant is a lifetime commitment, a promise of your will, not just between two people, but between a man and a woman and their God. Your marriage covenant involves three promises:

1. To stay married throughout your lives
2. To love and care for each other
3. To maintain sexual fidelity

You must enter into this marriage with a firm commitment to fulfill your marriage covenant. It is your covenant, your sacred unconditional commitment made in the presence of Almighty God and this company that will create a secure marriage relationship. Ellcot said, "Love is to will another's person's good." It is not based on feelings or emotions.

This idea is at the heart of commitment. You see commitment is willing another person's good through an unbreakable pledge of fidelity and devotion. It is an unconditional, irrevocable promise to always be there. It is the resolute convictions of your will to stick to that person for life.

When two people display that type of commitment in marriage, they freely fulfill God's purpose, and they become a witness to the world of God's character.

Commitment number 4: Becoming 1 flesh.

The phrase one flesh, (Genesis 2:24) is the origin of the term (oneness) that is why we say that in marriage, one plus one equals one. You see the one flesh in marriage is not just physical phenomenon, but a uniting of the totality of two personalities. In marriage, you are one flesh spiritually by vow, economically by sharing, logistically by adjusting time and agreeing on the disbursement of all life's resources, experimentally by trudging through dark valleys and standing victoriously on the peaks of success, and sexually by the bonding of your bodies. When you look at the place of becoming one flesh in Gods plan for marriage, it is clear that it should follow commitment- not precede it. It receives, leaves, cleaves, and then become one flesh.

As you and your spouse daily embrace God's plan for marriage, you will begin the process of becoming one. Something is born on every wedding day. Before the wedding ceremony, there is he and she. After the ceremony there is a new entity called, "us." This is the one flesh God speaks of a growing, thriving, living relationship.

In conclusion, when you build a marriage according to God's plan you will experience benefits that will enrich your lives. (Ecclesiastes 4:9-10) tells us, "Two are better than one because they have a good reward for their labor. For if either of them falls, the one will lift up his companion. But woe to the one who falls when there is not another to lift him up."

Everything I have talked about in this message, points to one central fact: for your marriage to become what God intended it to be, you must make a commitment to put God at the center of your relationship. For the heart of a oneness marriage is an intensely spiritual relationship between one man and one woman and their God. It demands a lifelong process of relying on God forgoing and enduring relationship according to His design.

_____ & _____ as a married couple to take charge of everything. I charge you both to take dominion over your property, each mate's spiritual growth, your children, your financial income and assets, as well as social and political influences. Take control of all earthly resources and be sure that they are used as God's spirit directs in order to bring honor to God.

You must remember God's charge to "subdue and rule." The earth includes not only the physical domain but the spiritual realm as well throughout the old testament and new testament, the Holy Spirit exults believers to be strong and courageous, (Joshua 1:6, 7, and 9.) To put on the whole armor of God, and to stand against the schemes of the devil. (Ephesians 6:11). Know this, that God is honored as we exhort victories in the spiritual realms for the sake of Christ.

Now that you know God's plan for your marriage, I charge both of you, as you approach this sacred ritual, to love and to live with a heart that is pleasing to God. The one who created you, who sent Christ to die for you, the God who loves you to the end. For God is unchanging, Jesus Christ is the same yesterday and today, and forever. His plan for your marriage is the same today as it was for Adam and Eve. You must believe it; you must follow his plan of oneness in marriage and experience abundant living. Let us pray.

Total Trust

Luke 23:46

"And when Jesus had cried with a loud voice, he said, father, into thy hands I command my spirit: and having said thus, he gave up the ghost.

The word, "commend" means to entrust for care or presentation. When Jesus said "father into thy hands I commend my spirit," he entrusted his father with the most precious possession he had, and that was his very spirit, to care for it, and to preserve it for him until he was with the father again. Listen church there were many things in our lives that we entrust to other people with no real guarantee of the outcome or the results. For example, we trust banks to keep our money, once we deposit it. We trust our jobs hoping at the end of the week we will receive a paycheck. We trust doctors with our health, hoping that they know what do for us to get us well. Ladies trust the beauty shop and men trust the barber shop to do a good job on their hair. We trust other people to do things for us and take a chance hoping that all goes well.

You know most of the time, we trust others more than we trust God our creator, even God has told us to trust in the Lord with all your heart, and lean not to our own understanding, in all our ways acknowledge him and he shall direct our steps. However, it is just simply human nature to trust others more. However, the relationship of trust between Jesus and God is something that we as people of God need to emulate. Even though God has brought us through many storms in our lives. A story is told about a young man in conservation with his father said to him, all that I am is because of Godly lessons that he (his father) had instilled in him. For that he said he would be grateful.

So, the question is, just how much do we as people of God, trust God in our lives. We say that we are born again Christians, but how much do we trust God? Do we trust him in the little things or do we trust him in all things? We should trust him in every aspect of our lives from the smallest to the greatest things that we deal with in our lives. As Jesus said before he gave up the ghost, "father into your hands I commend my spirit." We should also commend our spirits to God while we are yet alive. As all of this changed when Jesus died. The curtain in the temple which had signaled separation for God was now torn in two as a symbol that God is present with us. The work of Jesus on this earth was complete as he died committing his spirit to God his father.

The last word of Jesus shows us that he released his spirit to God. He was obedient to God, dying on the cross to take away the sins of the world. He dies for our salvation. John 3:16-17 tells us, "For God so loved the world, that he gave his only son, that whosoever believe in him shall not perish, but have everlasting life." For God, did both send his son into the world to condemn the world, but to save the world through him. The last word of Jesus reminds us that he was deeply connected to God and commended his spirit eternally. Our prayer should be, "Lord teach us to trust you more with all that we have, for all have come from you. For you are our creator and all that we are is because of you, we commend our spirit to you knowing that God will always take care of his children for you said that you will never leave us or forsake us. The song writer declared that, "I trust in God where I maybe upon the land or on the rolling sea for come what may, from day to day, my heavenly father watches over me." I trust in God. I know he cares for me on mountains bleak or on the stormy sea: the billows roll, he keeps my soul. My heavenly father watches over me. May God help all of us to live so close to God here on earth that we can commend our lives, our souls and spirits into keeping in the name of the father, son and the holy spirit, Amen.

Is God Really in Your Life First?

Focus Text: Matthew 6:33

"But seek ye the kingdom of God and his righteousness and all these things shall be added unto you."

Are you ready for an outpouring of God's power into your life? Do you need reviving in your soul? Well, if you answered yes to both of the questions, this is your wake-up call. God, by his spirit, has been speaking to the hearts of believers over and over and it seems as if they have fallen into a deep sleep. God is calling you back to a place of putting him, God, first in everything in your life. If you want to experience the blessings of God, then you must obey.

1. Well, what lessons can we learn from this sermon? First, many want to partake of the blessings of God, but they do not want to pay the price, which is in this case, obey his word. You must understand that there is "no free lunch," any place. There is a price that must be paid for anything you achieve

in your life. If you want to achieve great things in your life you must be willing to follow God's plan that is guaranteed to lead to victory. The only way you are going to know his plan is to spend time with him. For he knows all about you. There is a definite plan that God has developed for your life. His plan is far more superior to anything that you could ever create for yourself. With God as your senior partner, you are destined for success. Yes, you will have to work and become persistent with your actions. But praise God, you will know that your labor will not be in vain. God is going to do exactly what he has promised in his word. The more you allow him to take full control over your life, you can expect him to do, "exceedingly abundantly above all that we ask or think, according to the power that worketh in us."

2. We can have victorious living, Paul said in I Corinthians 3:21, "All things are your." The Christians I have met and talked to are always expressing the desire to living a victorious life, but do they seek God first? They are always seeking new ways to lead to victory. "All things are your," wrote, Paul, out of a more varied experience of great hardship and suffering of life that most people ever had or will ever expect to endure. You see, Paul experienced hate, persecution, being harassed for the cause of Christ. Being hungry and always confronted with an uphill climb that he might fulfill the promise to preach the gospel to all who would listen. All things are yours," whether life or death, or things present or things to come; all are yours, for who are you? You are Christ's and Christ is God. You see once you gain this kind of faith as a child of God, you can have a victorious life,

because Jesus Christ has done something for us. He hath made it possible that we can overcome Satan and his host. "Thanks be to God which giveth us the victory through our Lord Jesus Christ." I Corinthians 15:57 That is if we seek God first, which means to put God first in your life.

How to live victoriously? By fully believing in Christ as our Savior, admitting and surrender to his unmeasured claim on us, and be obedient to his word, commands and statutes. We can live victoriously and have abundant life because Christ works through us, therefore, all good works by us must be of and through Christ first. Only when we try to live the divine life can Christ manifest himself through us and lives in us. When the works of Christ is manifested through us there is no doubt that we have reached the point where we can begin to live the abundant life and be victorious. When we submit to his will, accent his love and believe in him first.

3. Finally, you must believe his word. For our God is more than enough God. He has promised to supply your need, but he wants to go beyond what you could ever expect. He wants to pour out an abundance of blessings upon you. He is able to perform miracles in and through your life. If you would just turn your life over to him. You see, turning your life over to him requires you to realize that you live and have your being in him. Everything that you will ever accomplish will happen because of God. Therefore, you are consistent in spending time with the one that is going

to bless you beyond what you could ever ask or think. Listen church. There is no one else who is able to do what God can do in and through your life. He is willing and able to take you to a height that you never believed possible. What are you waiting for? The time is now. It is later than you think. This could be your last wake up call.

God wants to do great things through your life. Will you let him become your number one priority? Will you seek him first and be obedient to him first? Well, only you can determine the kind of relationship you have with your heavenly father. If it is less than total surrender then you are cheating yourself. Seek him first with your whole heart and live abundantly. Become determined to know his plan for your life. When you heard from him, then walk in that which he has ordained for you. Get ready to go higher and higher in the Lord, and live the abundant life, by "seeking first the kingdom of God and his righteousness and all things will be added unto you."

In conclusion, the Lord makes a covenant with his followers. He says, "In effect, if you will put God's interest first in your life, I will guarantee your future needs. If you seek first the kingdom of God and his righteousness, then I will see that you never lack the necessities of life." This is God's social security program. The believer's responsibility is to live for the Lord, trusting God for the future with unshakable confidence that God will provide. Our job is simply a means of providing for our current needs; everything above this is invested in the work of the Lord. We are called to live one day at a time: Tomorrow can worry about its own things. Just seek him first and all things will be added unto you.

Dr. Gloria Bledsoe Cox, Biography

Gloria Bledsoe Cox was introduced to Jesus Christ through the New Hope International Ministries campus ministry at Illinois State University in the late 1970's. Since 1981, she has been a member of the NHIM under the prophetic and apostolic ministry of Bishop Harold Dawson, Sr. and the late Evangelist Mattie P. Dawson. Gloria served in many capacities at NHIM which includes being the Superintendent of Christian Education.

Gloria became the associate pastor of New Life Christian Church in 2011 under the leadership of the late Bishop Harold Dawson, Jr. She serves as a member of the board of directors and oversees various auxiliaries. She is currently the interim co-pastor with Pastor Spencer Gibson, Jr. for New Life Christian Church. Gloria is a member of the Purple Hat Battalion (PHB), an ecumenical prayer ministry, since its inception in 2006.

A devoted and passionate advocate for education, Gloria accepted a special education teaching position with the Peoria

Public Schools. She worked as a teacher and administrator for 35 years before retiring in 2014. She is currently working as a novice teacher supervisor for Bradley University.

Gloria dedicated most of her life as a lifelong learner. Her educational background includes Bachelor of Science in Education, Master of Science in School Counseling, Certificate of Advance Studies in Education Administration, and Doctor of Education in Education Administration. Gloria is creature of habit. All of her degrees were obtain at Illinois State University in Normal, IL.

Gloria was the wife of the late Deacon Albert Cox.

Gloria considers herself as a servant leader. She is an individual who understands the assignment of being a servant of the people.

The Fixer

---

2 Samuel 9: 6-7 (KJV)

6 Now when Mephibosheth, the son of Jonathan, the son of Saul, was come unto David, he fell on his face, and did reverence. And David said, Mephibosheth. And he answered, Behold thy servant!

7 And David said unto him, Fear not: for I will surely show thee kindness for Jonathan thy father's sake, and will restore thee all the land of Saul thy father; and thou shalt eat bread at my table continually.

Introduction:

God is able to fix that which is broken (disenfranchised, disillusion, dysfunctional families, disturbed society, broken marriages, etc.) so that what stands repaired is immeasurably greater than that which stood before it needed repair. Therefore, the most staggering brokenness conceivable is in reality the greatest opportunity imaginable. — Craig D. Lounsbrough

In this narrative, we see three known characters and a place. The characters are King David, Ziba, and Mephibosheth. The identified place is Lodebar.

1. First character is David. At this juncture, he is now King David. King David was a man after God's own heart (I Samuel 13:14). Who is this man named David? A man who started his journey as a lad of 14-16 years old who had an encounter with a giant. At a young age, he was anointed to be king over Israel. He was the shepherd boy who fought the bear and the lion, a fine musician, a writer who wrote the popular psalm — Psalm 23, a person pursued by King Saul, developed a friendship with Jonathan, became king, an adulterer with Bathsheba, and the murderer of Uriah. With all that being said, this David wanted to show kindness to any of King Saul's family for Jonathan's sake (II Samuel 9:1). Jonathan and David had a strong relationship, a strong bond; they were as close as brothers.

As a matter of fact, it was Jonathan who made a covenant with David in I Samuel 20:15, 16, 42 between their seeds. A covenant is an agreement which signifies a mutual understanding between two or more parties. Jonathan made David swear or give an oath for either one would show kindness from their house. During biblical times, a covenant was taken serious. There was loyalty, honesty, and integrity that stand behind the agreement. I remember as children, we did so- called blood covenant. We would prick our fingers, coagulate our blood, and shook hands. Or, we would spit in the palm of our hands and shook in agreement. Of course, we can't do those types of agreements today for health reasons, but the point is your word is your bond. In the case of David, he wanted to show kindness toward Jonathan's heir because of the covenant he had sworn to. God constantly shows kindness toward us — Romans 5:8 says, But God commendeth His love toward us, in that, while we were yet sinners, Christ died for us. David was informed that Ziba who was King Saul's servant knew the whereabouts of Jonathan's heir.

2. The second character is Ziba (II Samuel 9:2). Ziba was the servant of King Saul. After the death of Saul, Ziba seized his property. Ziba knew how Saul felt about David in regards to killing him. Ziba knew about Jonathan's son still being alive, the condition of the son, and where the son lived. But, he failed to tell David this information until he was brought before the king. Ziba had every intention to keep everything for himself.

3. The third character is Mephibosheth (II Samuel 9:6). Mephibosheth is the son of Jonathan and the grandson of Saul. He was crippled in both legs. He was dropped when he was five years old. It was customary in those days that when a ruler was defeated his entire family would be killed or put into slavery as well so that there would be no lineage of that rule left to proclaim the throne. David became king after Saul was defeated. When Mephibosheth's nurse got word that Jonathan and King Saul died, she took the child and ran. She was running from potential assassins. The

nurse feared that they would get the heir for the throne. She wanted to preserve they royal heritage. The nurse picked the child up because he couldn't run as fast as an adult. In her haste, she dropped him. The fall caused Mephibosheth to be lame in both of his feet. The fall changed his life forever. Not only did the fall crippled him in both feet, but crippled him in his thinking and his attitude about himself as well as life. Mephibosheth's condition was not of his own doing; no fault of his; the incident caused a misfortune in his life; life got the best of him; an accident occurred — he was dropped! Many of us had experienced being dropped or that we did the dropping. In either case it caused us to live in less desirable places and conditions. We were dropped, not by your own doing, with health issues (breast cancer), financial interruption (layoffs, reduction in the workforce, stock market crashes, and etc.), family issues (marriage, children), and social injustices. There are times that we are the cause of the problem. Either way of the dropping, there is good news! God is still a miracle worker. He is still on the throne. He is still a healer, a way maker, and a mind regulator.

The flood gates of life came open on Mephibosheth. The doors of low self-esteem, physical handicap, and shame brought on to him by his grandfather's sins. Many of us have experienced the flood gates open. The Word says, ...When the enemy shall come like a flood, the Spirit of the Lord shall lift up a standard against him (Isaiah 59:19). These types of issues are God's opportunity to show Himself strong in our lives. These are the type of problems that He comes in and fix. Due to Mephibosheth's condition, he found himself in a place called Lodebar.

4. The fourth point in this story is the place called Lodebar (II Samuel 9: 4, 5). Lodebar was a town in the Old Testament in Gilead not far from Mahanaim north of the Jabbok River in ancient Israel. He was in a place of nowhere. It was called Nothingville. The meaning of the town was having no pasture, no nourishment or green grass. It was a town of forgotten people including Mephibosheth. Lodebar was a place of lost people, unskilled people, uneducated, and outcast people. Here is Jonathan's son reduced down to nothing. Lodebar doesn't just inhabit poor people or the outcast, but it represents people who are disenfranchised, it represents people who are poor in spirit. Jesus said, "Blessed are the poor in spirit; for theirs is the kingdom of heaven." He said that he had come specifically to preach the gospel to the poor. We are finding people who are messed up on the inside although looking as if everything is alright. We are all familiar with the proverbial phrase, "You cannot judge a book by its cover. That is why we need Jesus in our lives. To allow the Holy Spirit to check, convicts, and console us.

5. King David sent word to bring Mephibosheth out of Lodebar. He did not need to be in that place. He is of royal blood. For every unbeliever, God is calling you out of this place. Every believer who is stuck in the wrong place, God is calling you out. You have been bought with a price. You

are a chosen generation, a royal priesthood, an holy nation; a peculiar people, that ye show forth the praises of him who hath called you out of darkness into his marvelous light (I Peter 2: 9).

6. In conclusion, getting out of Lodebar presents two blessings: 1) Restoration; 2) Redemption. In both of these blessings, good things are waiting for us when we get out of Lodebar. 1) Restoration: to return and give back something that was taken away or lost. Something that was once yours has now been returned. David took Mephibosheth out of the place of nothingness and returned to him all that belongs to him. In his restoration, Mephibosheth recovered all. Not only was he sitting at the King's David's table every night, but was to restore **all** the land of his grandfather. When you look at II Samuel 9: 9, 10, King David gave all of Ziba's property (which was Saul's) to Mephibosheth and told Ziba that he, his sons, and his servants will be working for him. 2) Redemption: the action of regaining or gaining possession of something in exchange for payment, or clearing a debt. David was clearing his debt. Mephibosheth became part of the family. In Romans 8:15-17, For ye have not the received the spirit of bondage again to fear; but ye have received the Spirit of adoption, whereby we cry, Abba, Father. The Spirit itself beareth witness with our spirit, that we are the children of God: And if children, then heirs, heirs of God, and joint-heirs with Christ; if so be that we suffer with him, that we may be glorified together. The King of Kings made us heirs.

God is able to fix that which is broken —whether you are disenfranchised, disillusion society breakdown, health issues, broken hearts, damaged emotions, crushed spirits, wounded bodies, and shattered souls. He is the fixer. He is getting you out of Lodebar so that what stands repaired is immeasurably greater than that which stood before it needed repaired. He fixed Mephibosheth, He can fix it for you.

According to Jeremiah 30:17, For I will restore health unto thee, and I will heal thee of thy wounds, saith the Lord; because they have called thee an Outcast, saying, this Zion, whom no man seeketh after.

This is what King David did for Mephibosheth, this is what King Jesus does for us. Jesus is "The Fixer" of our lives.

You Go-and Wake the Town and Tell the People

Matthew 28: 19-20: "Go ye therefore, and teach all nations, baptizing them in the name of the father and of the son and the Holy Ghost: (20) Teaching them to observe all things whatsoever I have commanded you; and lo, I am with you always, even to the end of the world."

Let me set the stage for you in which these words are spoken:

In these scriptures Jesus is in Galilee and He appears to His disciples as the risen Lord at an unarmed mountain. What a wonderful reunion this must have been His suffering was passed forever, because He lived, they too would live. He stood before then in his glorified body. They worshipped the loving, loving Lord, although doubts sill lurked in the minds of some.

Then the Lord explained that all authority has been given to Him in heaven and on earth, in one sense, He always had all authority. But here he was speaking of authority as head of the new creation. Since His death and resurrection, he had authority to give eternal life to all whom God had given to Him (John 17:2). He has always had power as the first born of all creation. But now that he had completed the work of redemption, he had authority as the firstborn from the dead "that in all things he may have the preeminence:" (Col 1:15 and 18)

Therefore, as head of the new creation, he then issued the Great Commission, which contained "standing orders" for all believers during the present phase of the kingdom, the time between the rejection of the king and his second advent. The Great Commission has three commands; they are not suggestions:

1. "Go, therefore and make Disciples of all nations." This does not pre-suppose world conversations, by preaching the gospel the Disciples were to see others become leaders or followers of the Savior from every nation, tribe, people, and tongue.

2. Baptize them in the name of the Father and the Son and the Holy Spirit. The responsibility rest on Christ's messengers to teach baptism, and to pass it on as a command to teach baptism be done and obeyed. In believer's baptism, Christians publicly identify themselves with the triune godhead. They acknowledge that God is their Father, that Jesus Christ is their Lord and Savior and that the Holy Spirit (gift) is the one who indwells, empowers, and teaches them. One name but in essence three persons: Father, Son and Holy Spirit.

3. 'Teach them to observe all things that I have commanded you." You see the Commission goes beyond Evangelism, for it is not enough to simply make convers and let them

fend for themselves. They must be taught to obey the commandments of Christ as found in the new Testament. The essence of Discipleship is to become like the Master and this is brought about by systematic teaching of the word of God and submission to the word. They must be taught so we must provide some teaching to them.

Then Jesus added a promise of his presence with His disciples until the consummation of the ages. They would not go forth alone or unaided but in all of their service and travel, they would know that the companionship of the Son of God was with them. Notice the four "ALL's" connected with the Great Commission: **all, authority, all nations, all things, and always**. Thus, the gospel closes with a commission and comfort from our glorious Lord. Nearly 21 centuries later his word have the same cogency, the same relevance, the same application, the task is still not completed, thus we must go. Wake the town and tell the people. What are you doing to carry His command?

Some said that there are three meanings or mode of communication: telegraph, telephone and tell-a-woman. Well, I don't know how true that is, but I do know that the Christian religion is a religion to be told about. For we have found something wonderful, a mind fixer, a heart, regulator, a comforter, a counselor, a God with us. We have to come to know Jesus as our bright and morning star, who is more wonderful than anything we will ever know. For Jesus is the best thing that could happen to you or me.

Several years ago, there was a song entitled, "Wake the Town and Tell the People." The theme of the song was, that a couple was in love and they wanted to tell the world about it. Oh, that we might wake up the whole world and tell them of the greater love of God. 1 John 4:7-21 tells us that God is love, the very embodiment of purest love. He loves us with a universal, sacrificial, redeeming love. The world and the church is sleeping and it needs somebody to wake it up and tell them. Well, if this is the case, who is it to do the telling? In the Bible, we are commanded to tell others what we have experienced. Psalm 107:2 says: "Let the redeemed of the Lord say so." The angel at the empty tomb of the resurrected Christ said, "Go and tell" Jesus himself said, "GO ye therefore, and teach all nations, baptizing them in the name of the Father, and the Son and the Holy Ghost; teaching them to observe all things whatsoever I have commanded you and lo, I am with you always, even to the end of the world. We as His disciples must do some telling.

Later, just before his accession, he said, "You shall be my witnesses unto me both in Jerusalem, and in all Judea and in Samaria and unto the utter parts of the earth." (Acts 1:8) Jesus was saying, you know me, you know who I am, you know what I've done and you have a message of redemption for the world, so don't you let the people continue to sleep, wake up the town and tell the people that God has always loved us, he always will love us, regardless of our faults and failures. For God love the good and the bad, the rich and the poor, the saints and the sinner, the educated and the ignorant. God loves us not just in word but in deeds. The Bible is full of his love. Thus, the climax of his love came about 2000 years ago, "For God so loved the world that he gave his only begotten Son, that whosoever believer in Him, should not perish, but have everlasting life." God loves a sinner, but has a peculiar love the one who comes to Christ. He loves him so much that he will never let him to go down into everlasting suffering. All through the Bible he makes the promise to all who will come and follow him John 1:12 says, "But as many received Him, to them he gave power to become the Sons of God, even to them that believe in His name." Let us wake up the town and tell the people that there is therefore now no condemnation to them which are in Christ Jesus, who work not after the flesh, no after the spirit; wake the town and tell the people "God so loved the world that He gave His only begotten Son, that whosoever beleiveth in Him, shall not perish but have everlasting life, for thou shall not perish but have everlasting life, for thou shall be his witness unto, all men of what thou has seen and heard.

Wake the town and tell the people how God brought you out of darkness into the marvelous light. Tell them how He save your soul one day, tell them how He's opened doors for you, and cared for you. Just tell them how he has blessed your life, be a witness for the Lord and you will fulfill your mission as s Disciple of Christ. Go and tell your story, It will wake the world and let them know that Christ lives within your soul as you keep your light shining for God gave it to you, use it to wake the town and tell the people.

Wake the town and tell the people that our mission is a life of service: How can we serve the Lord? We can serve Him by consecrated Christian living, by giving Him some of our time, by using our talents for the edification of his word on earth. We can serve him by giving of our tithes and offerings, by telling other of his love, mercy and grace and we can love him if we are faithful to his church. The best way for us to serve Christ is through his church. What do we owe the local church? We need to be full-service Christians.

Wake the town and tell the people that the mission minded means there is Christian activity in our life. Just as a physical body needs exercise for physical growth, so does the soul for need spiritual activity for spiritual growth. There are people who have been Christians for many year, but they haven't give much because they are complacent, satisfied with status quo and haven't engaged in any Christian activity. You always get out of a thing what you put into it.

A story is told of a preacher who took his son out to a country church where he was scheduled to preach. As they entered the vestibule, the preacher noticed and offering box. He dropped in a quarter. At the close of the service the church treasures said we always give our visiting preachers all the money we find in the offering box. So he opened up the box and gave the preacher the quarter. As they left the church the little boy said, "Papa, if you had put more in you would have gotten more out of it, wouldn't you?" That's true of our Christian mission and in the spiritual realm. We get out of it what we put in it. There are many of us who look food, but are doing nothing for the care of Christ.

We are the people who serve in the church and keep the Lord's work going. Not the great, the brilliant, the prominent people, but the faithful people. God can use even the least of us if we put ourselves in this hand.

In conclusion, you were not put on this earth to be remembered, no, you were put her for a purpose and to prepare for eternity. One day you stand before God, and he will do an audit of your life, a final exam, before you enter eternity. From the Bible we can surmise that God will ask us two crucial questions:

1. What did you do with Jesus Christ? Did you accept him as your Savior? Did you receive him of what he has done for you? Did you learn to love and trust him? For he is the way the truth and the light and no one comes to the Father except through him.

2. What did you do with what He gave you? What did you do with the light, your gifts, talents, opportunities, energy, relationships and resources God gave you? Did you spend them on yourself or did you use them for the purpose God made you for? You have a purpose tied up in a mission. God has his Disciples, wake the town and tell the people of Jesus.

God Chooses Just Plain Ordinary People to Serve Him

Joshua 2:1

Joshua 2:1 And Joshua the son of Nun sent out of Shittim two men to spying secretly, saying; Go view the land, even Jericho. And they went, and came into a harlot's house, name Rahab, and lodged there.

Introduction: The people of God should know and believe in the power of God as they view the conditions of this world. We hear each day stinging reports on the news, we read newspapers, the conditions of our cities, states and country, we see on the TV day to day conditions in our lives. We realize that life can be difficult even overwhelming and the problems that we face appear to be insurmountable. There are times that we view all of the confusion we experience and exposed to and wonder when it is going to come to an end. When is God going to intervene in all of this mess, when is God going to fix the chaos in my home? Therefore, I came to declare to you that God has already moved. God moved when he made us. Out of all the things God has done in the universe, have you ever considered the question, "Why did God make me? You must understand that God made each of us for a reason. There are many who try to bring you down and make you feel as though you are insignificant; make you feel as if your life doesn't matter; make you think that you do not even count. You do count. But that's not true. The devil is a liar, you do matter. You do count. There is something God wants for you. Not matter who you are, no matter where you have been, no matter what you have done or what kind of life you have lived, I came today to declare to you that God can use you. As insignificant as you may feel at times, that no matter who you are, where you have been, what you are or what kind of live you lived, God can still use you. The question is: Are you available to be used by God, will you allow yourself to be used by God and to become a servant of God?

In Romans 12:1-2, Paul tells the church at Rome, "I beseech you therefore, brethren, by the mercies of God, that you present your bodies a living sacrifice, holy, acceptable unto God, which is your reasonable service. And be not conformed to this world, but be transformed by the renewing of your mind, that you will prove what is good, and perfect and acceptable will of God." So, God wants to use you, but the question is will you make yourself available for him to use you? The song writer, William McDowell, put it like this: As he wrote and recorded the song, "*I Give Myself Away.*" The song says, "I give myself away so you can use me. Here I am, here I stand. Lord, my life is in your hands. Lord, I'm longing to see your desires revealed in me. I give myself away. I give myself away. Why? So you can use me. Take my heart: take my life as a living sacrifice. All my dreams, all my plans, Lord; I place them in your hands. I give myself away. I give myself away, I give myself away so you can use me." Then he continues to say, "My life is not my own, to you I belong. I give myself to you." I repeat that, no matter who you are, where you have been what you have done or the kind of life you have lived, God can use you, if you are willing to give yourself away for his use. How do I know? Well I am glad you asked? Because God used Rahab, God can use you. Do you know Rahab? The bible does not sugar coat who she was and what she was up to because in the second chapter of the book of Joshua, verse 1, it clearly says, "And Joshua the son of Nun sent out of Shittim two men to spy secretly saying go view the land, even Jericho. And they went, and came into a harlot's house, name Rahab, and lodged there." I think you know what a harlot is?! A prostitute! Therefore, I say it again, if God can use Rahab the harlot, God can use you. For God uses just plain ordinary people. Now what does ordinary really mean? It means, commonly encounters; usual. Of no exceptional ability, degree or quality, average or of inferior ability, degree or quality. Just an average. Then there are certain things that really doesn't matter to God, before he can use you. Anytime anyway. What lessons can we learn from this message?

1. It does not matter what your background is, God can use you. Backgrounds may mater to some of you, but your background does not matter to God. When it comes to us, we want to know, your last address, who you lived with,

your employment, your marital status, how long you lived at your current address. We even want to know your credit history, before we can use you. We want to know your educational attainment before we can use you. We even want to know the pedigree where you come from before we can use you. But what God wants you to know is, do you have a desire to be used and are you available? You see in God's sight, backgrounds do not matter. Regardless of who you are God is not concerned about where you been or where you come from. God is only concerned about where you are going. God is not in the least bit interested in what you did, or your past, but what I want you to know that God is more concerned about your future. God can use you, not matter how people have labeled you or how society has labeled you, God can use you. So, what, they called you an alcoholic, I want you to know god can use you. So, they labeled you a teenage mother, don't fret, god can use you. It really does not matter that they call you a drug dealer, God can use you. You may have even been called a gangster, a prostitute, an ex-convict, or a high school dropout, it doesn't matter what you used to be, God can use you, because backgrounds do not matter. I am so glad and thankful that all you have to do is come to him just as you are. For the songwriter declared, "Just as I am, without a plea, but that thy blood was shed for me, O lamb of God, I come, I come. I come not because I have been or I am perfect. I come not because I haven't done anything wrong. I come based on a promise that the bible says, "If anyone sins, we have an advocate with the Father,

Jesus Christ the righteous, and he is the propitiation for our sins, and not for our sins only, but for the sins of the whole world." (I John 2:1-2) So, God can still use me with all my sins, faults, and failures. What am I saying to you? God can use you. The word says, "If you confess your sins, God is faithful and just to forgive you of all your sins and to cleanse you of all unrighteousness. (I John 1:9) Therefore, God can use you because God has taken your sins and cast them into the sea of forgetfulness and he has placed on the seashore sign that say, "No diving here, now that stop some folk, but some people will get their spiritual scuba diving gear, their goggles, their snorkels, their flippers, and they will dive into the sea, pass by their sins and pick up your sins. But I'm thankful that even though they come up with your sins, "Jesus paid it all to him I owe, sin had let a crimson stain, he washed it white as snow." It does not matter what you use to do. All that matters is that you have a willing heart to be used right now by God. Yes, Rahab was a prostitute, but God used her. If you continue to read this text, not only do we find God can use you because your background does not matter.

2. God can use you if you believe in his miracles. Rahab was a prostitute, but she believed in God's miracles. The bible says, in verse 9, that when the men of Israel had come into the house and the pursers were looking for them, Rahab said to the men of Israel, "I know that the Lord has given you the land, that the terror of you has fallen on us, and that all the inhabitants of the land are fainthearted because of you. For we have heard how the Lord dried up the water

of the Red Sea for you when you came out of Egypt, and what you did to the two kings of the Amorites who were on the other side of the Jordan, Sihon, and Og, whom you utterly destroyed. As soon as we heard these things, our hearts melted; neither did there remain any more courage in anyone because of you, for the Lord your God, he is God in heaven above and on earth beneath." (Joshua 2:9-11) So it amazes me that as the children of Israel are camped outside of the city of Jericho, the city that was impenetrable, that before they were to enter into Jericho, they had to go through Jericho in order to get to the promised land. God sent them by Rahab's house because backgrounds don't matter. And he used Rahab because she believed in his miracles. That is the only credential you need, that you believe in God's miracles. I want you to remember that Rahab was a Canaanite. She was a descendent of Abraham, Isaac and Jacob, however, she believed in God's miracles. She did not come from Eygpt with the other Israelites, but she believed in God's miracles. Note that she did not cross the Red Sea on dry land, but she believed in miracles, nor did she experience manna raining down from the sky, but she believed in God's miracles, she did not experience drinking water from a rock, but she believed in God's miracles. Rahab heard about what God has done, and therefore based on what she heard, she was willing to believe in God's miracles. I wonder if there is anyone in the house who can believe in God's miracles. I wonder if you can believe in God's miracles, not only based on what you have heard, but based on what you know for yourself. I love Rahab because she said, "In spite of the fact that I am not a Hebrew, in spite of the fact that I am a Canaanite, I believe in God's miracles. He is God." (V 11) this makes it clear that she was a believer although she was a Canaanite; she was a woman of faith. If you don't believe that she was a woman of faith, just allow you fingers to do the walking through the bible and go to the New Testament Book of Hebrew, chapter 11. Look under the passage in the section of the Hall of Faith. There you will find the name of Abraham, Enoch, and Noah. You will also find among those other names, the name of Rahab, because she was a woman of faith. She believed in God's miracles. I'm authorized to tell you that God can use you. If you have faith, God can use you if you have enough faith to walk by faith and not by sight, God can use you. If you believe that, "All things work together for the good to those who love God, and those who are called according to his purpose. (Romans 8:28) God can use you. If you believe that God can still open blind eyes, God can use you. If you still believe that God can unstop deaf ears, God can use you. If you believe that God can still heal the sick, I mean Cancer, God can use you. All God requires is that you believe. For the word says, "For God so loved the world, that he gave his only begotten son that whosoever believeth in him shall not parish, but shall have everlasting life. For God sent not his son into the world to condemn the world, but that the world through him might be saved." (John 3:16-17) I came to declare to you that God can use you. If God can use Rahab, he certainly can use you.

3. My final point is that the world will be blessed by Rahab's ministry. Look at what happens in the text. It says in verse 12 and 13, "Now therefore, I beg you, swear to me by the Lord, since I have shown you kindness, that you also will show kindness to my father's house, my mother, my bothers, my sisters, and all that they have, and deliver our lives from death." So, because Rahab helped the spies, God used her, the world was blessed by her ministry. She said to the spies, "Be sure you remember my family." Her family was spared because what she did. Hold on, because it might shock you when I tell you this. Not only was Rahab's family spared but because God used Rahab, my family is spared. Because God used Rahab, not only was my family spared, your family is spared. How do I know this? Because God used Rahab in a special way. If you want to know how powerful of a way God used Rahab, as insignificant as she was, she appeared to have done or may have been. If you will look in Matthew, chapter 1, at the genealogy, and look at who begat who, eventually you will find there the name, Rahab. So that's right, Rahab's name is in the genealogy of Jesus. What does that mean; it means that in spite of the fact that she was a prostitute, God used her to bring forth Jesus. In spite of who you are, and what you have done, God can use you to bring forth Jesus. Rahab let God use her although she was a prostitute. No matter who you are and what you have done, God can use you. Please note that Rahab was not the first that God used in spite of what she had or who she was if you don't believe me let me call the roll.

144

Come here, David. What's that in your hand?" David said, "All I have in my hand is a slingshot and a smooth stone." But David, if you take that slingshot and a smooth stone and sling it one time for the Father, one time for the son, and one time for the Holy Ghost, the giant will fall down dead.

Come here, Noah. What's that in your hand? Noah said, "It's just gopher wood." But if you take a gopher wood and follow God's instructions and his architectural design, and build an ark, you can save your whole family, the nation and the world.

Come here, Samson. What is that in your hand? Samson said, "All I have is an ox goad." But if you use an ox goad, you can slay some Philistines to the glory of God.

Come here, little boy, with your lunch. What's that in your hand? The little boy said, "All I have is two fish and five loaves of bread." But if you give it to Jesus, he could feed a multitude with minimal resources.

Come here, Moses. What's that in your hand? Moses said, "All I have in my hand is a rod." But Moses, if you take that rod and stretch it over the Red Sea, the people can walk across it on dry ground and you will help me prove that I can be a bridge over troubled waters.

All you have to do is to allow yourself to be used by God. I came to declare to you in this house that God can use you, no matter who you are, no matter what you have done, no matter what you have, God can use you. "God uses just plain ordinary people who are willing to do what God commands. God uses people who will give their all, no matter how small it may seem to them. For little becomes much when you place it in the master's hand." If you do that God can use you to bring forth Jesus. All you have to do is declare one day, "I am thine O'Lord I have heard thy voice, and it told thy love to me. But I long to rise in the arms of faith and be closer drawn to thee. Consecrate me now to thy service now by the power grace divine: let my soul look up with a steadfast hope, and my will be lost in thine. Draw me nearer, nearer, blessed Lord to thy precious bleeding side."

Let your prayer be, "Use me, use me, spirit of the living God fall fresh on me. Melt me, mold me, and fill me." So Lord I am available to you for your service. Use me in the hospital, use me in your sanctuary, use me in the nursing home, use me in the church house, use me in my house, use me in the choir, use me as a deacon, use me on the usher board. Use me as a missionary, use me to work with the children and youth, use me to tutor or mentor, and use me to speak life." For if God can use Rahab, God can use you. No matter who you are, what you have done, when you did it, do not let Satan hold you hostage to your past: God is concerned about your present and your future. All that you have to do is give yourself away so God can use you.

I would like to close this message by reciting a song written and sang by Dannie Bell Hall in 1977, from her album title, "*Let Me Have A Dream.*"

Ordinary People

"Just ordinary People. God uses ordinary people
He chooses people just like me and you who are willing to do what
He command.
God uses people that will gave him all.
no matter how small your all may seems to you.
because little becomes much as you place it in the masters hand.

Just ordinary people (ordinary people)
My God uses (plain old) ordinary people (oh yes He does)
He chooses people just like me and you who are willing,
willing to do everything that He commands (oh yes)
God uses people that will give Him all
no matter how small your all might seem to you
because little becomes much as you place it in the Masters hand

Just like that little lad who gave Jesus all He had.
how the multitude was fed

with the fish and the loaves of bread what you have may not seem much but when you yield it to the touch of the master's loving hand, yes then you'll understand how your life could never be the same.

Understanding the Provisions of God

Rev. Dr. Freddie A. Banks, Jr.

Genesis 41:38-41.

38. "And Pharaoh said unto his servants, Can we find such a one as this, a man in whom the Spirit of God is? 39. And Pharaoh said unto Joseph, Foreasmuch as God hath shewed thee all this, there is none so discreet and wise as thou art: 40. Thou shalt be over my house, and according unto thy word shall all my people be ruled: only in the throne will I be greater than thou. 41. And Pharaoh said unto Joseph, See, I have set thee over all the land of Egypt."

Ruth 2:1-3.

1. "And Naomi had a kinsman of her husband's, a mighty man of wealth, of the family of Elimelech; and his name was Boaz. 2. And Ruth the Moabitess said unto Naomi, Let me now go to the

field, and glean ears of corn after him in whose sight I shall find grace. And she said unto her, Go, my daughter. 3. And she went, and came, and gleaned in the field after the reapers: and perhaps was to light on a part of the field belonging unto Boaz, who was of the kindred of Elimelech."

As I began to research this topic, I suddenly realized that all through my life and your life God has made provisions for us as we move from one situation to another. As we face our problems, as we make our career choices, as we try to accomplish our dreams, our visions, our aspirations, it is God who has already placed provisions within us. Each provision, God extends to us, is a gift received through Christ alone by faith alone. Therefore, Christ alone is our key to Christian living, for our dependence must be upon him, and what he provides for our lives.

Let's begin this sermon by first raising the question, what is meant by the word God's provision? It is the act of supplying the necessities of life from a stack of needy supplies. (To keep, maintain, support and take care of an individual and support them.) See God has already made provisions for us. We need to take them, no we just want to be strong and do things on our own, and yet a key principle in Christian life is that God is even stronger in His work than when we are admittedly weak, when we come to an end, he steps up and shows himself strong. God is provisionary, not a reactionary. He starts from a place of supply, not demand. When times are tough, the Lord is our only security. When days are dark, the Lord is our light. When our walk is weak, the Lord is our strength, yet, I have observed that we frequently have trouble believing God is our only hope, security, light, and strength.

Because we are so prone to try everything else, we automatically depend upon everything except the Lord. Yet He is still waiting there for us, patiently, to show Himself strong.

He is our light and our salvation, who should we fear? He hears our cry and provides. He lifts us up out of a horrible pit and make provisions. He places our feet upon a rock and establishes our going and provisions are made for us. He proves Himself strong in our weakness and provides. He sheds light in our darkness, He becomes hope in our uncertainty and security in our confusion. He is the centerpiece of our lives and there is only one prerequisite to obtaining God's provisions, we must be very sure that we truly know the Lord, that we have a relationship with the Lord, that we are new creatures in Christ Jesus and that we are born again Christians. Matthew 6:33 reads, "But seek ye first the kingdom of God and his righteousness; and all these things shall be added unto you."

Only then can we realize how God's provisions work in our lives, and how those provisions, each one of them, is a supernatural other resource permanently residing within your soul, ready for release everyday of your life on earth. People who do not know God, have no way of understanding the provisions of God. That is why they depend upon other ways of doing things, examples like; gambling, stealing, excessive labor and etc. It thus becomes our responsibilities to access God's provisions. Let's turn our attention to taking possession of God's provisions.

Accepting the Provisions

For example, let's first consider what God did for Joseph, because Joseph stayed true and faithful to God. Yes, he was sold into captivity, Genesis 37:3-28. Yes, he was a dreamer and his dreams created problems with his brothers. Yes, he was put into prison, Genesis 39:20. But God was with him. Protecting him, providing for him, even in an Egyptian prison. Ordinarily, a man would become bitter after spending years in prison. His prison experience led to an introduction of a baker and a butcher, which led to an introduction of the King to interpret his dream, because Joseph was faithful to God. God promoted him and made him Prime Minister of the greatest nation of that day, Genesis. 41:38-41. God's provisions were there all along. What his brother meant for evil, God meant for good to save a whole nation. God's provisions are there for us, we just need to be faithful and reach out and take possession of them.

Let's look at the book of Ruth 2:1-3 as another example of taking possession of God's provision. God has visited his people in giving them bread. (1:16) The blessing was in the field, but it did not erase the influence of the famine on the minds of the people.

The provision: God is a provisionary, not a reactionary, God starts from the place of supply not demand. The first verse in chapter two declares God's provisions, watch this, Boaz. "There was a relative of Naomi's husband, a man of great wealth, of the family of Emlimech. His name was Boaz." We are told that Jesus was the lamb slain from the foundation of the world. (Revelations 13:8) Prior to Naomi's need, the law declared the poor, the widow and the stranger were to be allowed to reap the corners of the field and to gleam the harvested field for personal provisions. The provisions were already there, but there was a problem.

Let's look at the problem: The narrative of chapter two implies that this law was not being obeyed. Influenced by their famine experience, the majority of the people were harvesting every inch of the fields and nothing was being left for the poor, the widows and the strangers. First, this is suggested by the fact that Naomi did not ask Ruth to go, but it was Ruth that asked permission from Naomi. Secondly, it is implied that Ruth hoped to find someone who would allow her to glean their field (v2) and asked permission to glean (v7). Apparently, gleaning was dangerous. The provision was there, but the purpose for that belonged to the poor was being stored as an insurance against another famine. This meant that the effects of the famine were still being felt by the poor, the widows and the strangers. In spite of visible evidence, Ruth sought the word of God. "So Ruth the Moabitess said to Naomi, please let me go to the field and glean heads of grain after him whose sight I might find favor." (2:1)

Taking possession of God's provision: The provision was in the field, but it had to be gathered. It took faith for Ruth, a Moabitess to step into hostile territory and claim God's provision. What am I saying to you who have vision, hopes, dreams and aspirations in the various ministries of the church: The only way to make your vision, your dream a reality and take possession of God's provision is by faith. You must begin to resisting Satan, in steadfast faith who claims that you cannot achieve it. For the victory that overcomes the world is, our faith. You want to take possession of God's provision by walking by faith and not by sight. You must remember that without faith it is impossible to please God. For God is pleased when we take advantage of the sacrifices that Jesus made for us to be free. Jesus gave us authority to overcome our problems, and he has made provisions for us, we just need to reach out and take possession of them.

For example, like the woman with the issue of blood, we must be determined to press past the barricades and the obstacles that stand between God's provision and us. Ruth had to overcome the famine mind set of Naomi, the fact that she was a Mobitress, and the reluctance of the locals to comply with the will of God.

Note, the Israelites had to dispossess walled cities in order to possess their inheritance. Jesus called the man at Bethesda to rise, by faith and obedience, take up his bed, and walk. If we are going to realize God's provision for us, then we must cease moaning and groaning about what we cannot do, about what we have done in the past, about what resources we do not have, and then we can do and use what provisions we do have and move forward.

For God's provisions are in the field and will become our possession only as we dare to lay hold of it. The modern church often forfeits God's provision because it allows unbelief and disobedience to determine what it will possess. Our churches are not doing anything because they have not taken possession of God's provisions. The religionist says, "It hasn't happened, so it can't happen." If we allow the sensationist to determine what God's will for us to do, we will live in famine conditions during the time of visitation. This is true of several NT provisions. Healing, Jesus said that healing was the children's bread. (Mark 7:27)

Baptism in the holy Ghost, the promise is unto all those that afar off. (Acts 2:39) Gifts of the spirit. We must let faith take hold of us and then take hold of the provisions of God by faith. This will involve persistence prayer.

Trusting providence: Ruth did what she could and left the rest to God. She went and gleaned in the field after the reapers. In addition to this we are told that she happened to come at the part of the field belonging to Boaz. Keep in mind that world shaking events often hinge upon apparently insignificant incidents. For example, the selling of slave boy, Joseph, to the Ishmaelite, turns out to be the salvation of a nation and the world. The capture of an unnamed little Hebrew maid made the difference in the cleansing of a leprous Naiman, running into Rabhab's house makes the difference between life and death for her and for her family. Ruth did what she could, took possession of God's provisions for that, she encountered the needed blessing, and the blesser.

God was visiting the people with bread, but what good is bread if we are not allowed to partake of it? Days of visitation will be no better than days of famine if we do not get up and take possession of God's provisions. The song writer declared that every promise in the book is mine, every chapter, every verse, every line, this is true, because the promises of God, turns out to be the way to the provisions of God if we take advantage of them. But it only becomes a reality when you or someone dares to take possession of God's provisions, for they are yours for the taking. Keep in mind that God is a provisionary, not a reactionary. He starts at the place of supply not demand. This is the third time that I have made this statement. God has already put people in your life who are part of God's provisions, open your eyes and see them. There are names and opportunities and open doors you so insensitively push shut because you did not see them as God's provisions. Let me call attention and ask you to remember how Mary and Martha expected Jesus to come to their home. But there was a difference in the expectation in how he would show up. Mary recognized him, the provision of his presence in him immediately when he arrived and she stopped everything including preparing the house for him to enjoy, experience and to learn from him. But Martha did not recognize that he already had shown up despite where she was in her own preparation for him.

Jesus spent most of his life here on earth being a breathing testimony, so never think you can figure out God or his system. I am certain Martha's attention on his living breathing presence in her immediate moment. I am also as certain he did not want her attention on practice, social etiquette, and religiosity. Instead she missed out on God's provision in her own space, because she had settled for someone's definition of how he would come.

What does this say to us? Make sure that you do not allow someone else to define how God will provide for you. His words to her stings my own soul. "Martha, Martha, you are worried and upset about many things, but only one thing is needed. Mary has chosen what is better and it will not be taken away from her." (Luke 10:4-42) I am not an anarchist; I do not want to miss God's provision for you. I don't want to walk along the edge of his order. I don't want to miss him, because I trust his order more than I trust mine. So, let my prayer always be, "God help me to see your provisions and take possession of them, help me to choose what is better and make me a Mary."

God provides in the time of need
He provides relief of stress
He provides assurance for worry
He provides strength for temptation
He provides peace for fear
He provides hope for trials
He provides grace for suffering'

He provides forgiveness for failure
He certainly provides all that I or you ever need

In conclusion, what you must do is make sure that Christ alone is our key to Christian living, and our dependence must be upon him and the provisions that he has for our lives. Place in your heart, that this day, you will reach out and take possession of God's provision. Then your vision that God has given you, the Pastor's vision that God has given to him, your hopes, dreams and aspirations can be accomplished and achieved with the provisions of God. Follow him and his vision and see God work is provisions in your life.

The Lord Gives and
The Lord Takes Away

Scripture Text: Job 1:19-21

Focus Text: Job 1:21 And said, "Naked came I out of my mother's womb, and naked shall I return thither: The Lord gave and the Lord hath taken away, blessed be the name of the Lord.

Today we are gathered here to celebrate the homegoing of ********. I am told that he was a believer who accepted Christ at an early age. He loved his family and friends.

To this family, we want you to know that we share your grief and your loss this day and our prayers are with you. As we come today to this solemn memorial occasion, to celebrate the homegoing of **********, we are reminded anew that our funeral services are not for the deceased but for the living. We are not here today to talk about life for he lived his life to the fullest and in essence he preached his own funeral. We are not here to judge the inner secrets of any person's heart for we do not know what emotions stirred his soul, nor do we know what secret communion he might have had with God as his own personal Lord and savior, master and redeemer. We do not know what personal encounter, experience, or relationship that he had with God. Therefore, my purpose and task as a minister of the gospel, is to try to bring a measure of comfort to the family and friends whose hearts may be heavy and burdened today. However, I do know that our God is a great and loving God, who never make a mistake. He always looks upon the heart of a person and He always knows and does that which is right, just, and best. So with confidence, we leave your loved one in hand of a merciful heavenly father. We thank God for him and we bless his memory. God has spoken to us through his life, and his character so today you should listen to what God speaks to us through his death. So much has already been said, that I believe what we need to do now is simply preach the word. I think that he would want the people that he loved to know God, to trust God, to have a personal relationship with God, and to walk with God, for I came to let each of you know that only a life in Christ Jesus is worth living. In preparation for this eulogy, my thoughts took me to the subject, "The Lord Gives and the Lord Takes Away," Job 1:21.

The possibility exists for you to misunderstand me when I say that there is a rhythm to life. The misunderstanding may occur if you assume that I believe the world operates totally as a cycle. History is not cyclical but linear. Life, the gift from God, is an unfolding saga that is moving into the future under the all-powerful eyes of God who is in control of all life. History is being influenced by God; therefore, we are not victims of a repetitive cycle. Yet even a casual observation of life indicates that a certain rhythm prevails in our existence. This rhythm does not signify the absence of God, but it is an indication of God's love as He and He alone provides the predictability to life. Our gathering here today is part of that rhythm. Our text refers to a man who knew God, but He also knew well aspects of life, He knew that there was rhythm to life, that included good and bad, it included joy and laughter, it included life and death. In swift succession, Job had lost property and his children. Yet, in the midst of his great loss, Job was able to rely on his faith in God and say, "The Lord gave and the Lord has taken away; blessed be the name of the Lord" (Job 1:21). You see, there is a divine rhythm of give and take to life. The Lord gives and the Lord takes away. In this setting, we would agree that all life is a gift from God. You are not here on our won, God has granted you the gift of life. Our daily existence is a reminder of the gracious gifts of our loving God. Our own life as well as life all about us, is not the evolvement of matter or a result of some cosmic accident. For the word says we are created in the image of God, we are precious in His sights, He has made us and created us for His glory and He loves us. Therefore, we have purpose and design from the Uncreated One. Job said, "The Lord gave." What does He give? Obviously, this physical life that you and I enjoy and yearn to maintain is a gift of God. God also adds quality to this physical life. Happiness is a gift from God. Even now, you recall many hours of happiness with this your departed loved one and friend. Happiness does add a quality of life, for happiness makes everything better. God gave us happiness that we might be better people, memories of happy events continue to warm us and motivate us. In the memorial service, there is another gift of God which we should not overlook. Saint Paul said, "Thanks be unto God for His unspeakable gift" (2 Corinthians 9:15). That unspeakable gift is the gift of salvation, made possible through Christ Jesus. God's gift of salvation through His son as the savior of the world is what makes life worthwhile. You see, it is being saved, knowing Christ as your savior, that actually brings joy into our lives. It is the gift of salvation that allows our setting today to become a type of celebration. Salvation is God's gift to dry our tears, because we know the Savior, whom we can seek. In times like these, we know God will lift the burden of death from our hearts. He will come to comfort all who mourn. Death would be an unbearable experience were it not for God's gift, but because of Him there is hope. We must come back to Job. He also said "The Lord has taken away." We have hardly listed all these gifts from God, when we are reminded of this setting. God has taken away. There are many losses in life, but now comes the greatest loss. The Lord has taken a loved one, and death has invaded a family. a loved one has been take away. If we truly believe that God created life, then we must confess that He has the right to do with life as He so chooses. Through this life of our friend, He has shared a precious gift. He has called that life home to be with the Lord. In the process of doing so, the appearance is that God has taken back His second gift. That of happiness. No one expects you to be happy when saying good-bye to someone who is very special. Because God has been with us in Christ, He knows the sorrow of losing a loved one. It is easy to be trapped and misled into believing that there is no happiness in death. We are primarily aware of tears and troubled hearts. We may even wonder if God has forsaken and forgotten us. Then we remember His third gift which He has never recalled an suddenly everything begins to look different. As we remember the gift of salvation, hope shines through the gloom. Even though God has called home a life and tears are real, in Christ Jesus we have a salvation that is steadfast and sure. Overachieving and undergirding our gathering here is the fact of salvation. If we see through the eyes of our faith, we can join Job and say, "Blessed be the name of the Lord." While the appearance is that physical life and happiness have been taken back, salvation through Christ Jesus has not been recalled. The Lord gives, but He does not take all His gifts back. We must remember that all of life is in the hands of God. Faith will help you overcome grief which flows from the rhythm of our days. Through strength from our faith, we can say with Job, "The Lord gave, and the Lord has taken away. Blessed be the name of the Lord." Because we are human, we grieve here and now. May we show the confidence of our faith by our personal testimony as we say, "Blessed be the name of the Lord." I realize that the family, friends and loved ones have all been affected by his death. In the mystery of life, our tenuous threads have been interwoven through his life. Each one of you need to be upheld by God's powerful love, however you must know God, you must have a relationship with God, experience God, and be accepted and saved by God before you can be upheld, comforted by God's love as you gather for this funeral to mourn. Keep in mind that God has not abandoned you. He has not forgotten you either. But know this, that grief makes discouragement and depression common ailments. Makes no difference how much you pray, fast, anoint with oil or touch and agree. Death and grief causes our souls to be downcast and our faith to ebb thin. And as the deer pants for streams of water, so our soul begins to long for God even as we ask why. Yet this is the good news. Your loved one came. God gave him life for years and allowed him to share that life with you. But he was never fully ours, for God is yet in charge. Creation's mystery has been completed and his days among us we think may have been too short. But the influence of a life spent upon earth is realized by the length of time spent here. The energy of life is valued by how many others it touches. Many of your lives have been touched by him and because of his influence, many of you will never be the same. For God sent him to linger momentarily among you and the messages that he spoke have yet to be revealed. For the Lord gave and the Lord has taken away and blessed be the name of the Lord.

Let us pray…

Lord, you have given, and now you have taken from us. Even in our grief and pain, we continue to call you "Blessed". For giving us the life of this dear soul and the gift of many memories, we offer our thanks. Most of all, for the gift of eternal life, which is never taken away, we offer out thanks. In Christ's name, Amen.

You Don't Have to Be A Pilate

Isaiah 53: 4-5

Good Friday Service

Once again, God has spared us to come to the Edge Easter. By God's grace and mercy we find ourselves living during another Easter season.

You cannot approach this sacred moment without being reminded of Jesus and his disciples, Peter, James, and John, when he led them to a high mountain. There, before them he was transfigured, He was changed. Peter recognized that something great, something important had happened; thus he said to the master: "Lord, it is well that we are here: if you wish master, I will make three booths (tabernacles here, one for you and one for Moses and one for Elijah" (Matthew 17:4 RSV).

If I might use the words of this disciple, I say to you: It is well that we are here today, not to build three tabernacles, but we are here to look introspectively into our lives. We are here to search our Christian character to see how we can improve it. It is well that we are here to work on this building the one that is not made by mortal's hand.

I pray that God will grant us the vision to see ourselves through the character, the faults, and failures of Pointus Pilate. May God then save us from Pilate's path of futility and lead us fully unto his service. For Jesus has set before us certain responsibilities and tasks, that we cannot escape. You see he did not command us to be like Pilate, but to be unlike him. Therefore, each man is called at least, to the task of being responsible of standing firm in those things which he believes that are righteous, honest, and just. As

Jesus said: "Not my will but thine be done." To follow any other path is to lose your purpose in life.

If I was a painter, one of the subjects I would like to put on canvas would be that of a lost soul. For I believe there is no sight more horrible, no soul more confused, than that person whose life is drifting down paths and streams of nothingness.

Pilate was such a person who followed this path, who failed to stand firm in right things. Pilate was the fifth governor of Judea. And to history, certainly to Christianity, he would have meant nothing except that our Lord and Master stood before him to be judged; our Lord worked, suffered, and died under this man.

Like a mighty blacksmith, striking his heavy hammer against a hard anvil, Pilate struck the blow; he issued the order, though silently, that condemned Jesus. He was you might call the trigger to the tragic, yet glorious, occasion.

We recognize the fact that he should not bear all the blame, for there were others in this drama of human suffering. Caiaphas, the high priest, must stand as the plotter, Judas as the deceiver, and the soldiers as executioners, all must be found guilty too. Regardless, each man, each person, must be responsible for his own personal conduct, his own divine destiny.

Men throughout history have asked: Why did Pilate surrender Jesus after finding him not guilty? Why didn't he stand up for what he believed? Did Pilate really believe that he could wash the guilty stain from his life by merely saying, "I am innocent of this righteous man's blood?"

I realize that man has no right to judge his brother. Yet man's failures and successes are judges by the tracks left upon the sands of time. History reveals that Pilate was a man who thought he could carry a bucket of water on each shoulder, without spilling a drop.

For instance, when Pilate was first appointed governor of Judea, he allowed his soldiers to establish idolatry within the Holy City, then Pilate removed the image of his God from Jerusalem. In other words, any man who kicks his own God out because of criticism, because of opposition. Is a man of weak conviction? He is Pilate.

In the second place, Pilate wore a robe of instability. He trod the path of indecision he was not a Nicodemus who wanted to be changed. He was not a Nicodemus who encountered Jesus in his personal life. By the water and the spirit, Pilate was not a Paul, who met his master on the Damascus road. He was not a Martin Luther or a Martin Luther King Jr., for that matter. He would not say, "Here I stand, God have mercy on me."

Pilate was like many of us, like many of us on the church rolls. He thought he could please everyone and God. How often we Christians drift upon this cloud of impossibility and are carried by these winds of instability and indecision.

When Jesus was accused by the priests and officers of the Sanhedrin, Pilate refused to be moved by the charge that Jesus was a disturber of the peace. Here He had his chance to be a Nicodemus, to be transformed, but acting true to his pattern, when a more powerful charge was made against Jesus. He gave up. When Pilate was put on trial too, when his life was in jeopardy, when his exalted position was challenged, he was torn asunder by indecision. He just couldn't make up his mind.

The only way he saw out of his maze was to escape making a decision by sending Jesus to Herod. But again he failed to find an escape over the path of futility. However, Pilate got a second chance, Herod forced him to do something with Jesus. For a while Pilate held firm. But when the unrelenting bigots would not retreat, he allowed Barbados to go free and Jesus to be crucified.

He had turned over individual His responsibility to other people. He acted as though it was not his decisions to make. Did he have the authority? Did he not sell his birthright? Surely Pilate suffered a severe breakdown in human personality: FOR HE HAD SINNED. His sin let him think that he was innocent. Instead he should have cried out, like this Negro spiritual: "It's not my sister or my brother, but it's me O Lord. Standing in the need of prayer." Or, it's not the crowd, but it's me, Pilate, standing in the need of prayer.

We as Christians even today, face the same act of history as we seek to release Barrabas and to crucify Jesus daily. As we face a confused, frightened mankind, needful of God's love and understanding, we often forsake the real self, the spiritual being in us, and leave our destiny up to the desperate, crying, crowds, crying out, "Crucify him, crucify him" Jesus.

No longer then is the master of life on trial at Jerusalem, but we are all on trial: the bigots, the human courts, the shallow compromises, the laws and yes even the church stands at the bar of divine justice, with Jesus as the real judge.

Therefore, we are confronted with two powerful and important questions as we seek to walk in the path of righteousness.

There is the question the governor asked the crowd. The question that still echoes through the corridors of times, even unto generations yet unborn: "People what then will ye do with Jesus?" The other query resounds under the listening sky to each of us, is what then will you let Jesus do with your life?"

Make no mistake about it, Pilate could have been forgiven, made whole. For there is a hope for all of those who like sheep, go astray. As Jesus would say, "Father, forgive them, for they know not what they do." Father, forgive Judas, my betrayer. Father, forgive Pilate, the judge too. Teach them the power of love, which is the real value of life.

You see Pilate's anxiety to avoid offense to Caesar, his God, to save himself from, harm certainly did not save him from political disaster. The power he loved was gone; the prize he sought was lost. As Jesus would say, "What does it profit a man, if he shall gain the whole world, and lose his soul?" Too often, we are like Pilate. Governor Pilate did not gain the whole world, and yet he lost his soul.

Well, what happen to this confused and this sinful man? Well tradition takes up this drama where the Bible leaves off. It claims that Pilate sought to hide his sorrow on a mountain somewhere near Lake Lucerne. And even though he spent many years on that mountain, in deep remorse and despair, he never really repented. Just as though he had not wasted a good life by following the path of vainglory, he added to it another sin by plunging himself into the dismal lake near the mountain to complete his death, to end that leads nowhere.

I am sure that anyone with a forgiving heart, with a Christlike spirit would have found himself, somewhere along the road, would have found himself before it was too late. I am sure many Christians would hope that Pilate could have been another Nicodemus, who was there to help Jesus down from the cross, to help bury his body in the tomb; or if he could have been like Paul, or even like Judas, the betrayer, who repented before filling his grave. But no, Pilate took the wrong path home, the road of futility.

Well, as I take my seat, my Christian brothers and sisters, I want you to know that this story is told over and over, not because it is new. For really it is old as the flow of blood in your human veins. It is told because it concerns us, it concerns our lives. For even today the church of Jesus Christ stands before the governor. Even today each of us is on trial. We still hear the ancient questions pounding in our ears. "Whom shall we release?" "Or, what will we let Jesus do with us?" "Or, what will we let him do with me?"

Now let me tell you that the reply is not Pilate's any longer, but it is ours. As we decide, not once, but every second, every day of our lives, in every experience, let us not be afraid to serve the Lord. Let us not be afraid of making real sacrifice in his name. let us recommit and rededicate ourselves to his keeping. Don't be afraid or ashamed to do great things for God, with God. And certainly for God's people.

As Isaiah, the prophet, wrote centuries ago when he was encouraging his people, today we hear him saying, "surely he has borne our grief, and carried our sorrows." For if God has done this once, and I know he has, certainly God will still continue to grant his grace and mercy to those to those who serve well. God loves those who serve him. Therefore, let us follow him all the way, from earth to heaven, even though it will be a cross.

Jesus assures us: if anyone wishes to be a follower of mine, he must leave self behind. He must take up the cross and come with me. Whoever cares for his safety is lost; but if a man will let himself be lost for my sake he will find himself (Matthew 16: 24-25).

And finally brethren, quoting from Albert Schweitzer's, the quest of the historical Jesus: "He meaning Jesus, comes to us as one unknown, without a name, as of old, by the lake side, he came to those men who knew him not. He speaks to us the same word: "Follow thou me." And sets us to the task which he has to fulfill for our time he commands. And to those who obey him, whether they are wise or simple, he will reveal himself in the toils, the conflicts, the sufferings, which they shall pass through in his fellowship."

For You Don't Have to Be A Pilate, in the name of the Father, Son, and Holy Ghost.

Isaiah 53: 4-5 RSV: "Surely he has borne our grief and carried our sorrows. But he was wounded for our transgressions he was bruised for our iniquities, upon him was the chastisement that made us whole, and with his stripes we are healed.

Do You have a Passion for His Presence?

Psalm 42:1-6 NIV

As the deer pants for streams of water, so my soul pants for you, O, God. My soul thirsts for God, for the Living God. Where can I can and meet with God? My tears have been food, day and night, while men say to me all day long, "Where is your God?" These things I remember as I pour out my soul: How I used to go with the multitude, leading the procession to the House of God, with shouts of joy and thanksgiving among the festive throng. Why are you downcast, O my soul? Why so disturbed within me? Put your hope in God, for I will yet praise him, my Savior and my God.

Tonight/Today as we open this 180th annual conference, let's look at this passage and focus on the subject "Do you have passion for his presence" Several years ago, there was a gospel song that was recorded, that seems appropriate to me as we talk about worship. Donald Lawrence and the Tri-City singers recorded this gospel song with Daryl Coley as the lead singer. It said in essence:

When Sunday comes, I feel my best.

There's something that happens in me when Sunday comes.

I know I can go to church.

I know I can get to the house of the Lord.

I can get to the place where I can worship the true and Living God, when Sunday comes.

I don't know how you feel about Sunday, but there is something special about Sunday to me. There is something very special about the gathering of the people of God. Something special about coming into the House of God and worshiping god with everything that is within me. I like to see the smiles on the saints' faces when a song is sung that they enjoyed. I like seeing a rejuvenated or lifted heart when a scripture is read that a person really resonated with. Have you ever been in church and heard a word that almost seemed tailor-made for you? Have you come to worship service and it seemed like the preacher knew all of your business? It seemed like the entire worship service fit your situation; it seemed as what was said forked for your circumstance. It seemed like everything that went on that day was all about you and you wanted to know: Who's been talking about me to the preacher? Who's been telling my business? Who told the preacher about what's going on in my life?

Isn't it interesting how the Holy Spirit can tailor-make things just for you? Isn't it interesting how the word of God can seem to be fashioned just for you? And when you are thinking that the service is just for you, there is somebody on the same pew saying, "That was just for me." It is amazing how the Holy Spirit operates and makes everything work out just so that we can go home refreshed, renewed, and revived. We can go back with a sense of having been in the presence of the almighty God. The Bible says, "That is his presence there is fullness of joy and at his right hand there are pleasure forevermore." Psalm 16:11

Therefore, when I come to church for worship service, I expect to feel better on the way out than I did when I came into the house. You see, there ought to be something that was sung. There ought to be a handshake, a hug, a mile, and a kiss that changes my situation when I come into His presence. Whereas, I came in with my head hung low, I ought to go back out with a smile on my face and a testimony that God is able to do all things well. When I come to church, that is really what I expect. I expect to feel better because I have been in the presence of the Almighty God.

You see worship is not about the people: It's about God's presence. It's not just about being on a certain pew: It's about being in the presence of the Almighty God. Brothers and Sisters, we need to have a passion for God's presence. We need to have a passion for God so strong within us that is moves us so that Saturday night we get ready for church. We don't wait until Sunday morning to decide what we're going to wear to church. You don't wait until Sunday morning to get your things in order. We need to get things together before church so that we can enter into His gates with thanksgiving and into His courts with praise (Psalm 110:4). We ought to come to church ready for revival. In fact, revival ought to happen every time we get here. We should expect to be rejuvenated every time you come. Even if the word of God challenges us, we ought to be better because of that too. Even when it doesn't fit what we think is the right thing, we are better because we have been in the presence of the Almighty God.

I believe that's what is going on as we approach our focus text Psalm 42. Let's look at this text to see what lesson it might have for us. The Psalms are some of the best literature, some of the best- written material we can ever find. The Psalms speak to every life experience. They help us to understand how people really go through circumstances, through a trial, and the variation of changes and vicissitudes of this life. We can think about every aspect of life through the eyes of the Psalmist. It is interesting how we can look through these Psalm and even see ourselves in them. We see their battles and our battles. We see their tremendous obstacles and challenges, and we see ours. We see their enemies and their trail, and we see ours.

All of us at some point in our lives can resonate with that thing called an enemy. Everyone can remember, we can reflect on some time in your life when you had to deal with an enemy. And that's what is going on with the Psalm we chose this morning. This Psalmist is frustrated. The Psalmist is concerned because as much as he enjoys worship, he cannot get to the Temple of the Lord to worship, as he desires. As much as he loves going to church, as much as he looks forward to coming into the presence of the most high God, as much as he looks forward to being in the Temple, in the sanctuary, he can't get there because his enemies are so fierce (sickness) that he is barred from Temple worship. That's a horrible thing, not to be able to get to church and you want to get to church. That is a horrible thing to be exiled from the house of the Living God; you cannot get to the church. Has anybody been in this situation before?

This is bitter reality. He says, "I need to be in the presence of the most high God. Look at what he says, "As the deer pants for streams of water, so my soul pants for you, God." He says, "my soul is long for the Living God. In other words, I need to get in contact with my God. I need to be in the place where I know god is in residence and is active. I need to get into God's house and feel his presence and experience his joy and know his peace and again feel his salvation and delight in his deliverance. I need to get there. I need to get into his presence. I need to know that he is mine and I am his and to feel him moving inside of me.

Have you ever had that kind of feeling where you knew that you were right where God was and you knew that you and God had a thing going on? Have you ever been where you had the presence of God saturating you all over, engulfing you? It is a wonderful things to know that God is all over you and moving through you and in you. The Psalmist says, "I long for that," and he uses a water image. He says, "I am dehydrated because I cannot get to my source, "The first thing that I gleam from the 1st verse of the Psalm is that the Psalmist makes being in the presence of God a priority. He puts reverence as a priority in his life. Reverence is not something that is on the back burner for him. Reverence and worship is not just something that happens once a week. Worship is something that's a priority for him. Let me ask you, have you prioritized worship? Have you made worship a top priority in your life or do Sundays just come and go? Is the opportunity to be with the people of God just another stop during the week?

Or, do you have a need, a longing to be in the presence of God, or is it just something you do because decent folk do it? The Psalmist says this is not just something I do for shape, fashion or form. This is something that is high on my life of priorities. This is a necessity. Worship is a requirement. Worship is also something that I choose to do, and that's how worship ought to be for all of us. You ought to be so in tune with God. You ought to love God so much, there ought to be such an intimacy between you and our God that you can't pass up a day of worship. You just cannot allow a day to pass without being in the presence of the most high God. Worship must become a priority for you. For the Psalmist said, I need worship. He said, "My soul thirsts for God, for the Living God. Where can I go and meet with God." Why can't I go to church? Why can't I get to the temple? Well my friends, I need to push us on this piece a little bit. I understand that we need to come to church as much as we can so we can be in the presence of God and God's people. For the Bible says, "Forsake not the assembling of yourselves together." We need to be in church, but is this not the only place we can worship God or comes into his presence? This brings us to our second point in worship.

1. I believe the Psalmist had a misunderstanding of this whole notion of worship. He says, "When can I go and meet up with the Living God? When can I get to the temple?" He unfortunately has so localized and centralized the presence of God that he feels he's got to get to church to be in the presence to be in the presence of the most high God.

    He has made God a narrowly restricted God. He has made God a parochial God, a God who exists only within four walls, a God who can only be found on a plot of ground, in a certain locale. But somebody in here has been walking with God long enough to know that it really doesn't matter if you can get here or not. Because I come to tell you this morning if you have a true relationships with God, and He is the head of your life, you can worship God anywhere. I come to tell you and help you understand that the worship of God is not about a place. To worship God is about a person. Worship of God is not about where, it is about WHO you are worshiping. Worship of God is not about geography. It is about intimacy. So when I worship God, it does not matter where I am. For I can worship God in a full house, in an empty house, in a poor house, or when there is nobody around. I can worship him without a piano. I can worship him if a chord is never struck on an organ. If there anybody who has read John 4 and you know that worships is not about where we are; it is about who you are in communication with. Therefore, somebody knows that I can worship God on my way to church and sometimes that's our worship. For if you cannot worship by yourself, you cannot worship at all, because there is something about just you and God in a holy hookup that makes all the difference in the world. Is there anybody in this house today who knows about this holy connection.

2. Let's turn our attention now to a 3rd reason to worship since we know it ought to be prioritized, and it can be done anywhere. If God never does anything else for you other than save your soul and provide your salvation, you still ought to have a lifestyle of worship and a reason for His presence. Listen church, if everything goes crazy in your life once you leave this house this morning, you still ought to be a person of worship. Even if things don't go your way,

you should still know who God is and what god is capable of doing and that ought to make you worship Him. Can I get a witness?

I believe the three Hebrew boys made that plan plain for us. They said even if our God does not deliver us, we know he is able to deliver us. And so we won't bow before anybody else. We will only bow before the true and living God. We will only adore the true and Living God. We will only adore the true and Living God, and it doesn't matter what kind of idol you emit. Our God is still worthy of our worship and nobody else. The great African theologian, Augustine, said that God has made us for himself and our souls cannot rest until we find rest in him. I'm sure that somebody understands what that means. You have tried a lot of things: You have tried a lot of people, but you realize that can't nobody do you like Jesus. You have been a lot of place, and you have been in a lot of circumstances, but you don't want any in your life more than Jesus. Is there anybody in here who just got a love affair going on with the Lord? Is there anybody in here who can't help but love God, can't help but worship Him?

You wake up in the morning thinking about His goodness. You can go to bed at night thinking about His goodness and His greatness. You just stop in the middle of the day and take a praise break because you realize how awesome and wonderful God is.

I've got a longing to get back to God, my soul thirsts for the Living God. Where can I go and meet my God? You don't have to go anywhere. You can stay wherever you are and hookup with God. You can be any place and at any point in your life and know that you can meet up with God. But this is not the end of the story.

3. This Psalmist also had a frustrating time because his enemies begin to taunt him, said, "uh, uh, so you can't get to church. You can't get to worship. Tell us where is your God now? You are in this horrible situation, but where is your God now?" It's right there in Verse 3; the folks want to know where is your God now, now that you have gone through all that you have gone through. Now that you are in the circumstance that you are in right now? Have you ever had circumstances that taunted you like that?

    The Psalmist is in deep-seated depression. He doesn't know how to handle what he is dealing with, and all of this is teasing and taunting begins to frustrate him even more. Where is your God? You have been tithing and it seems that you don't have enough money to pay your basic bills. Where is your God now?

    You have a debilitating disease that you can't get rid of. Where is your God now? Your children are strung out and hung up. Oh, Lord! Where is your God now? Every now and then circumstances will taunt you like that. Every now and then situations will get to you like that but I'm glad this Psalmist had at least prioritized reverence and worship.

But not only did he prioritize reverence, in Verse 4, he begins to help us a little bit more. He said, "These things I remember as I pour out my soul." He vents, he complains, it's a lament. He is frustrated, but he says, "These things I remember as I pour out my soul. I remember how I used to go with the multitude leading the processional to the home of God with shouts of joy and thanksgiving among the festive throng." He says situations are bad right now.

Circumstances are not all that pleasing now, but in my depression, in spite of this mood of melancholy, in spite of the difficulties that I face right now, I have a personal reflection that allows me to begin to remember how things used to be. It may not be right for me now, but I remember when God was my rose of Sharon, my Lilly of the Valley, when my God handled the last situation that I had to deal with. Things may not be as well as I would like for them to be today, but I remember a time when I used to go to church. I may not be able to get there right now, but I used to lead fold in to the house of God, and I remember the shouts of thanksgiving and the praise that I lifted up when I went to the house of God.

And even though I can't get there now, I am going to just let my mind take me back, and I am going to begin to reflect on what God has already done for me.

And so my brother and sisters, you are going to have to do that sometimes. You are going to have to get in that kind of posture every now and then. Because on this journey, there will be sometimes when you can't find anybody to say a good word for you, but if you can let your mind take you back to the last time that God made a way, I believe there is something about seeing what God has already done that will give us strength to know that God can do it again. Is there anybody in this house this morning who knows that God majors and minors in repeat performances? Our God is able to do it again. If He did it for you once, He can do it again. Our God is an awesome God, and we worship Him and we adore him and we magnify him because He is able to do it again.

4. In conclusion, there is one more things: There is power in this text. I see the Psalmist who has prioritized reverence. He puts worship first. But I also see how he takes time for personal reflection. He begins to think about what God has done, and if you only use your mind for forward thinking and never for backward reflection, you are not using the totality of what God has given you. God has done so much for us. Every now and then it behooves us to take some time out and think of His goodness to us.

So when we get to Verse 5, the Psalmist begins to talk to himself. I like this, because most folks say you are crazy when you talk to yourself. But, the Psalmist begins to talk to himself. Look what he says, "Why are you downcast, O my soul? Why are you so disturbed within me?" He says, "You have been reflecting on what God has done, so I dare you to be still downcast. I dare you to still be disturbed," The Psalmist says, "I will yet praise him, my

Savior and my God." I like that. Every now and then you ought to get a "Yet" praise point in your life. Yet I will praise him. He begins to talk to himself. David said he encouraged himself in the Lord, because sometimes you won't find anybody to encourage you. Sometimes you cant find anybody who will talk for you. So every now and then, you will have got encourage yourself. Folk get tired of dealing with you after a while. They say when you come to them over and over again, you are trying to make them codependent. So folk don't want to be bothered. Go ahead and talk to yourself. "Self, get yourself in order!" Put our hope in God! For God has done for you before. Don't you know that He will do it again? So, yet will I praise the Lord.

I don't know about you brothers and sisters, but I've got my hope in God. I don't know how things are going to work out in the future, but I know who holds the future, and if He holds the future, He is able to handle my future and me. Is there anybody in here today who understands the power of holding on to God's unchanging hand?

And so the Psalmist has prioritized worship. He took some time for personal reflection. But lastly, because of his personal reflections, he has a powerful rejuvenation. There is something, brothers and sisters, to think about what God has done. There is something about going back, letting our mind, think back that does something for you that would never been done just by asking somebody else to pray for you because you know your story better than anybody else.

And so, when I get into his presene, even if I come dejected, even if I come depressed, whe I just think about what God has done, something in me starts to move and something in me starts to get busy and I get rejuvenated in worship. I refuse to go back the same way I came. I refuse to go back with my head held down. Thank you Lord for giving ease to my troubled mind. And the Psalmist says that if you will yet praise him, God will do for you what nobody else can do. Will you yet praise him? Will you yet worship him in spite of? Id there anybody here who's got a passion for his presence? Then you ought to help me praise God! You ought to lift up your hands and praise Him for there is power in your praise.

- Regardless of what is going on…yet will I praise Him.
- Sickness in my body…yet will I praise Him.
- Finances-money struggles (Lord, I don't know how I'm going to make it)…yet will I praise Him.
- My family don't understand me and what I'm going through…yet, will I praise Him.
- I've got some trials and tribulations in my life…yet will I praise Him.

For I hear my mother's voice as she sings:

"I want Jesus to walk with me. All along this pilgrim journey, I want Jesus to walk with me. In my trials, walk with me; in my trials, Lord walk with me. All along this pilgrim journey, I want Jesus to walk with me. When I am troubled, walk with me, when I am troubled, Lord walk with me. All along this pilgrim journey, I want Jesus to walk with me."

About the Book

We find ourselves in the most vulnerable and troublesome situations as Christians, but God has put forth good news in Meditational Moments with God: Sermons for Reflections and Spiritual Growth Volume II.

Used as a personal guide or as a reading, Mediational Moments with God: Sermons for Reflections and Spiritual Growth Volume II is to be shared with Christians and mon-convents and is sure to be treasured by any person seeking enlightenment or encouragement. This inspiring work presents several highly versatile meditations designed to enhance your relationship with God through the study of His word. Each Mediation is prefaced by an appropriate passage from the scripture, spackled with story illustrations, and is spiritually oriented to provoke spiritual thought.

Designed to inspire, comport, console and aid others, Mediational Moments with God: Sermons for Reflections and Spiritual Growth Volume II will speak to all believers and strengthen your relationship with the Lord Jesus Christ.

About the Author

Dr. Freddie A. Banks Jr. was the pastor of Samuel Brown Temple A.M.E. Zion Temple in St. Louis, Missouri for 14 years and the pastor of Unity Christian Fellowship Ministries Zion Church at Eastern Illinois University in Charleston, Illinois for six years. He holds advance degrees from Southern Illinois University College of Education. He is a profound educator in his roles as a teacher, principal, district Superintendent and university Professor. He received the Outstanding Elementary Educational and Community Service Award in 1972 and the previous recipient of the Duquoin Chambers Lifetime Achievement and Rotary Presidential Award. He is worked in the Duquoin School District for 24 years before he decided to aid student from all walks of life at John A Loan Junior College. He has authored many articles in educational journals and assisted in a grant program that aimed to recruit and retain minority students into teaching positions while employed at Eastern Illinois University. His previous works include: A Determined Soul, with God you Can Make It; The Plight of the African American Male-We Can't be Silent; Meditational Moments with God, and Mediational Moments with God: Sermons for Reflections and Spiritual Growth Volume II.

Printed in the United States
by Baker & Taylor Publisher Services

Printed in the United States
by Baker & Taylor Publisher Services